HEAL THE LAND

Reflections on a corporate prayer journey
for the transformation of Stoke-on-Trent

Robert Mountford

*To Dave and Sandy
With grateful thanks
for your fellowship

Robert
5/11/11*

Stoke-on-Trent
2011

Tentmaker Press
121 Hartshill Road
Stoke-on-Trent
Staffs. ST4 7LU
www.tentmakerpress.com

ISBN 978-1-901670-69-1

Front cover:
An original painting by Shelagh Powell.

CONTENTS

PREFACE

I offer this book as a personal reflection on the corporate, seven-year journey of humility, repentance and prayer that began in Stoke-on-Trent ten years ago. The Experian report of September 2001 labelling the city as the worst place to live in England and Wales was the spark that led to the birth of a prayer movement for the transformation of the city.

The Bible verse that became the focus of our journey was 2 Chronicles 7:14, in which the Lord says 'if my people, who are called by my name, will humble themselves and pray and seek my face and turn from their wicked ways, then I will hear from heaven, I will forgive their sin and will heal their land.' Our goal was throughout, and remains, the 'healing of the land' of the City of Stoke-on-Trent.

I insert a practical comment at this point to clarify that, while the City of Stoke-on-Trent was the focus of the Experian report, and of the prayer journey related in the book, there was a natural and strong interaction between people/churches in the City of Stoke-on-Trent and those in the neighbouring Borough of Newcastle-under-Lyme, and in the surrounding areas of Stafford Borough, the Staffordshire Moorlands and South-East Cheshire. Stoke-on-Trent may have been the first target area, but no limits were ever placed on involvement in the corporate journey. In the book, therefore, the phrase North Staffordshire is used to refer to the wider area which connected with the prayer journey.

This is a personal story, in that I, along with my long-standing friend Lloyd Cooke, was at the very heart of the journey recorded in the book. Together Lloyd and I led almost every public meeting, chaired every private discussion and read/wrote every e-mail connected to the prayer movement. We were there before day one and there after this leg of the journey had come to an end. Whatever criticism may be laid against this book, it cannot be said that we do not know the subject matter. I am greatly indebted to Lloyd, without whom the story recorded in this book would not have contained the blessing, nor experienced the progress, that it did.

This is a corporate story, in that it is shared by hundreds of people from across Stoke-on-Trent, North Staffordshire and beyond, who participated in the holy moments of prayer and praise, and who prayed sincerely and sacrificially for the healing of the land. Friendships were built, people were encouraged, hope was stirred, humility was fostered, vision was imparted and faith was stimulated as we met together around our common goal. Without the commitment of so many people for so long, there would be no story to tell.

This is an inclusive story, in that it crosses historic boundaries between different groups of people who share the geography of the city in common, but whose paths may not have crossed before the prayer journey began. This book relates how Christians from different backgrounds found each other, how people of faith came to pray for secular leaders, and how city leaders re-engaged with the church. Old ways of thinking, believing and behaving were either blurred or removed in the wave of repentance and prayer that overtook us.

This is an incomplete story, in that there is still a long way to go before the 'land' of Stoke-on-Trent is fully healed and restored to God's purpose for it. While those of us who were involved in the prayer journey are extremely thankful for all that we have received, we acknowledge that the foundations for something new may be laid, but the building has yet to be completed. This may mean that there are more books to write…!

This is an illustrative story, in that the principles we have learned in our journey in Stoke-on-Trent relate not only to this locality, but are applicable in other towns and cities similar to, or dissimilar from, Stoke. I have made every effort, therefore, to base the story in the reality of time and place, but also to draw out the principles and values which can be applied in any and every location.

I am very grateful to Mike and Ev Carter, Steve Ellis, John and Brenda Redfern, and Linda Williams and the Seedbed team, without whose practical encouragement and support this book would not have been written. Debra Green, leader of Redeeming our Communities, offered valuable advice about the layout of the book, for which I am also grateful.

I dedicate this book to my son Christopher, daughter Anna, daughter-in-law Kate, granddaughter Molly and grandson Joel. You are the future of our family and, along with others, of the great City of Stoke-on-Trent. I pray that the foundations being laid will proceed to completion and so enable you to live in a society transformed by and to the glory of God. Finally I thank my wife Sue, for her total commitment, encouragement and support in more than 30 years of marriage. Sue, you are my rock.

Robert Mountford
2 September 2011

FOREWORD

Your people will rebuild the ancient ruins and will raise up the age-old foundations; you will be called Repairer of Broken Walls, Restorer of Streets with Dwellings.

(Isaiah 58:12 NIV)

What will it take?

City transformation is now being experienced all over the globe as the Spirit of God moves in power from within the Body of Christ, out to local communities and into the marketplace. Such transformation is currently evident in most continents around the world, with the exception of Europe.

So, what will it take to bring revival and God's glory to our towns and cities here in the UK? This question has exercised the thoughts of leaders in Stoke-on-Trent over the last decade as God has led us on a significant 'foundation-laying' journey. While there will always be an element of the sovereignty of God, I believe that there are three vitally important keys that will be central to such a move of God.

Prayer

Although it takes more than prayer to see a breakthrough, without prayer there will be no birth and what is birthed will not be sustained. Prayer brings about great changes, and I am most grateful that God is a God who hears and answers prayer. We also need to remember and acknowledge that many breakthroughs are going to come, not because we have prayed, but because the prayers of previous generations are awaiting an answer in our time. Central to such prayer is repentance and this was the starting point for the Body of Christ in Stoke-on-Trent back in 2001. As Pentecostal pioneer Frank Bartleman said, *'The depth of your repentance will determine the height of your revival.'*

Leadership

A lack of city-wide leadership can also be debilitating to progress in seeing the purposes of God released. We talk much about church leadership but little about town-wide or city-wide leadership. Key to developing such thinking is remembering that we need to exchange the concept of leadership in a church or a city as being 'leadership over' for the concept of leadership being 'leadership within'. Jesus himself said that his followers were not to lord it over and that he was one who was among them to serve (Luke 22:25-27). We need to rediscover commitment not just to our 'parish' but also to our 'conurbation'. We need leaders who not only focus on the promise found in Jeremiah 29:11 of a personal 'hope and a future,' but who will also embrace the corporate call to *'seek the peace and prosperity of the city'* (Jeremiah 29:7).

Unity

Importantly, underpinning both prayer and leadership is the third key, unity: we need united prayer and united leadership. While Psalm 133 highlights the vital importance to God of unity, it does not necessarily mean that we all express our Christianity in the same way. I believe that God is looking for a unity that is expressed in an even greater level of diversity.

However, such a city-wide focus on prayer, leadership and unity will undoubtedly be costly. In his book *The God Chasers* Tommy Tenney writes,

> He wants us to press in for His secret things. Often He will stop our attempts to build monuments to partial and incomplete revelations of His glory. We like things to come quickly, easily and cheaply – microwave revival. Many modern saints spend a lot of time looking for shortcuts to God's glory. We want the gain without the pain.

Spiritual maturity is always determined by our willingness to sacrifice our own desires for the interests of the Kingdom or for the sake of others. The door that requires the most sacrifice to enter will always take us to the highest level.

I warmly welcome and commend this book from my good friend, Robert Mountford. We have journeyed together in Stoke-on-Trent for over twenty years and were both privileged to facilitate the 2C7 prayer network. The lessons we learned have been the source for this book's inspiration. This is not a book of theory, but is one forged from experience, through nights of interceding and crying out to God and blended with a clear Biblical perspective. My prayer for all those of you reading this book is that we might renew our commitment to praying and working for greater unity – the glory of God in our towns and cities may be at stake!

Lloyd Cooke
Chief Executive, Saltbox Christian Centre

...if my people, who are called by my name, will humble themselves and pray and seek my face and turn from their wicked ways, then I will hear from heaven, and I will forgive their sin and will heal their land.

(2 Chronicles 7:14)

1: THE WORST CITY

Exactly two weeks after the explosive and world-changing events of '9/11', when Islamic terrorists hijacked four American aeroplanes and flew them into the Twin Towers of the World Trade Centre in New York and the Pentagon in Arlington, Virginia, a report on the state of the towns and cities of England and Wales was published on Tuesday 25 September 2001.

Experian report

Experian, a national Information, Analysis and Credit Agency, had compared and ranked the 376 towns and cities of England and Wales according to eight indices – retail activity, quality of schools, house prices, unemployment rates, nett weekly disposable income per household, number of cars, level of motor crime, household theft and density of population.

Residents of the areas of Uttlesford (Essex), the Malvern Hills and South Norfolk were undoubtedly pleased to learn that, according to the chosen indices, they enjoyed the best quality of life in the country. Residents of the North Midlands City of Stoke-on-Trent were less than pleased to discover that their city was reckoned to be the worst place to live in England and Wales.

Following publication of the report, local radio stations BBC Radio Stoke and the independent Signal Radio leapt to the defence of Stoke-on-Trent, as did the daily newspaper, the Sentinel. Letters poured in to the newspaper from local residents and former residents, as well as from civic leaders and visitors to the area. Most spoke passionately about the friendliness of local people, about the wonderful heritage of the pottery industry and about the famous people born and raised in the area.

For its part, the Sentinel newspaper launched the 'Proud of the Potteries' campaign, complete with posters and car stickers for those who wished to make a public display of affection for their city. Award-winning, Stoke-based reporter Dave Blackhurst produced the most strident response to the Experian report, writing in the Sentinel, 'Once more we have the hub of the universe (otherwise called Stoke-on-Trent) under fire in a study which would do the back of a fag packet an injustice.'[1]

Rich heritage

Despite such displays of anger with Experian and passion for the city, Stoke-on-Trent was facing numerous deep, wide-ranging, ongoing challenges at the dawn of the 21st Century. These economic, educational, social and political challenges were not unique to Stoke-on-Trent. Most, if not all, similar towns and cities in the Midlands and North of England which had, like Stoke-on-Trent, been born out of, and/or shaped by, the Industrial Revolution were also facing major issues concerning the future.

The fundamental question for Stoke-on-Trent was simply, 'Now that the industries which built the city have relocated to other parts of the world, what does the future hold for us in terms of our identity and purpose? In Stoke-on-Trent, the strong, particular industrial flavour had been a mixture of coal-mining and pottery, supported by a smaller, but

[1] Response to the Experian report by Dave Blackhurst, *The Sentinel*, Tuesday 25 September 2001, page 3.

important, iron and steel sector. Much of the output of the iron and mining industries had been used to support the central and largest industry – pottery. Pottery had for centuries been produced in North Staffordshire in any and every form - tiles and toilets, sinks and baths, cups and saucers, teapots and ornaments. Hundreds of small 'pot-banks' had employed thousands of people, since the industry was traditionally labour-intensive and the workers wary of mechanical help.

So huge became the size of the pottery industry and so great the fame of the pottery made in the area, that the name by which the city was best known to the world was 'The Potteries.' No other city in the country had a name which was as synonymous with its principal product in the way that Stoke-on-Trent was. It was the 'pits and pots' that had brought work and people to the area, causing a sustained increase in population during the 17th, 18th and 19th Centuries. The population of the area that is now known as Stoke-on-Trent grew by a full 800% between 1801 and 1901. The growth was not only rapid, but unplanned and chaotic. It was only during the second half of the 19th Century that the six main towns which had resulted from the population explosion were incorporated, bringing a modicum of health safeguards, public amenities, administrative organisation and justice into the equation.

The six Pottery towns of Tunstall, Burslem, Hanley, Stoke-upon-Trent, Fenton and Longton (to name them in order from north to south) were federated to form the County Borough of Stoke-on-Trent in 1910, in what was the largest such federation to take place in British history. The County Borough was elevated to the rank of City by His Majesty King George V during his visit to Stoke-on-Trent in June 1925.

Challenging history

The pottery that made the city famous throughout the world, however, was produced at huge cost to local people, because foundries, coal-mines and pot-banks were labour-intensive and highly dangerous places in which to work. Each work-place involved long hours of toil, had poor lighting, was filled with dirt and dust, and suffered from a lack of ventilation. Many employees were involved in lifting heavy objects, while for some there was the intense heat of the foundry, coal-mine or the bottle-kiln to contend with. In earlier times, women and children were involved as much as men and boys in both coal-mining and pottery. It was not uncommon for boys and girls to begin work at the age of six. All who worked in either the 'pits or pots' were especially likely to suffer from respiratory afflictions such as asthma, silicosis, emphysema and pneumoconiosis.

It was not only the working conditions that were dangerous. Housing standards, diet and sanitation were also poor, while families were large. Overcrowding was common and drunkenness rife. The physical atmosphere itself was dirty and dangerous, the result of hundreds of bottle-kilns pouring out smoke day and night. Weeks could pass with no sign of sky or sun, due to the thick pall of smoke hanging over the area. Not surprisingly, infant mortality and sickness rates in the conurbation were always higher than the national average and life expectancy was considerably lower.

Christian faith

Christian churches played a significant role in the life of the Potteries towns throughout their history, especially during the formative period of the 18th and 19th Centuries. In the 19th Century, dozens of Church of England parishes were carved out of the historic Parish of Stoke-upon-Trent in an attempt to keep pace with the burgeoning population. After a long period of exclusion, Roman Catholic parishes were also established, especially in the second half of the same century. However, it was the non-Conformist Christian churches which exercised the greatest influence over the character of the people and the development of the towns that would later become the City of Stoke-on-Trent.

The Methodist movement was introduced into the area by John Wesley, who, with his brother Charles and friends such as George Whitefield, made it his ambition to 'reform the nation, by spreading scriptural holiness over the land.'[2] The early Methodists pursued this goal by committing themselves to a methodical lifestyle of prayer and fasting, of Bible study, of helping the poor and needy, and of spreading the Gospel of salvation in Jesus Christ whenever and wherever they found opportunity to do so.

Unlike other Anglican clergymen of the time, John Wesley did not confine himself to Christian work in one parish, but travelled extensively over a 50-year period. Wesley visited North Staffordshire on 16 occasions between 1738 and 1790, where his main local base was at Burslem. Though experiencing opposition to his Gospel preaching for many years, towards the end of his life Wesley was witnessing a genuine revival of Christian faith in the Pottery towns.

In March 1787, 84-year-old Wesley rode on horseback into Lane End,[3] at the southern end of what is now Stoke-on-Trent. He recorded in his journal for that day;

> ...we entered into the country which seems to be all on fire - that which borders on Burslem on every side;

---

[2] John Wesley, in 'Minutes of Several Conversations Between Rev. John Wesley and the Preachers in Connextion with Him.'

[3] Lane End is known to us as Longton.

preachers and people provoking one another to love and good works in such a manner as was never seen before.

Later that same day Wesley led a large and powerful meeting in Burslem, during which several people were converted to Christian faith. He wrote;

> Indeed, there has been, for some time, such an outpouring of the Spirit here as has not been in any other part of the kingdom; particularly in the meeting for prayer. 15 or 20 have been justified in a day. Some of them had been the most notorious, abandoned sinners in all the country....[4]

Powerful revivals

Following John Wesley's death in 1791, Methodism splintered into separate factions. Two of the most prominent of these groups were intimately connected to the towns of North Staffordshire. New Connexion Methodism did not begin locally, but it found its national centre in the area. Its flagship church was Bethesda Chapel, situated on the south side of the town of Hanley. A first chapel building was erected in 1808 to house the burgeoning congregation, but a larger building was soon required. In 1818 a 3,000-seater chapel building was erected, possibly the largest non-Conformist chapel building in the world at the time. Throughout the 19th Century, the leaders, trustees and members of Bethesda Chapel exerted a powerful influence on the town of Hanley.

Another influential Methodist group, known as The Primitive Methodist Connexion, had its origins in the northern fringes of North Staffordshire in the early years of the 19th Century.[5] The descriptive title 'primitive' was based

---

[4] Recorded by John Wesley in his *Journal* on 29 March 1784.

[5] Specifically in Tunstall, Kidsgrove, Harriseahead, Newchapel and Mow Cop.

on the group's aim to rekindle the spiritual passion of Whitefield, the Wesley brothers and the original ('primitive') Methodists some 60 years previously. Solidly working class in its constituency, passionately exuberant in its worship and aggressively evangelistic in its outlook, the Primitive Methodist Connexion developed strong and extensive roots in the area. It grew rapidly throughout the first half of the 19th Century and reached from North Staffordshire into every corner of the British Isles – and far beyond.

The impact of these various Methodist groups on the people of the Potteries was both intensive and extensive. Methodism moulded the personal character of generations of citizens. A good Methodist was committed in worship and prayer, self-disciplined in attitude, temperate in character, moderate in outlook, hard-working in business, careful with money, yet generous to the poor. Methodism also shaped the collective culture of the area. The spiritual vision embraced in the chapels was disseminated by education in the form of Sunday Schools. Social cohesion was strengthened by means of chapel-related choirs and sports clubs, while political aspiration found expression in the form of trades unions.

Successful evangelists

Other influential leaders from Methodist backgrounds also impacted the towns of the Potteries in the 19th and early 20th Century. Phoebe Palmer, Richard Weaver, William Booth, Gypsy Rodney Smith and Edward Jeffreys each experienced great success in the area. Weaver, Booth and Smith would also later speak publicly about the formative impact made upon them and their ministry during the time they spent in North Staffordshire.

In 1882, at just 21 years of age, Gypsy Smith built a congregation of 10,000 people in Hanley in just six months from a standing start. He would leave Hanley in 1887 to embark on a 60-year career as a world-travelling, internationally-famous evangelist. Wherever he preached, whether in Australia, South Africa, Europe or the United States of America, Smith would recount stories of his time in the Potteries. As if to seal the special connection, Smith named his younger son, who was born during his time in the area, Hanley Smith.

Edward Jeffreys, an evangelist from South Wales, was to turn the then-new City of Stoke-on-Trent upside down in the autumn of 1930. Edward conducted a series of evangelistic and healing meetings in the major town halls in the Potteries. In a social context of extreme poverty and hardship, Jeffreys' healing missions offered a beacon of light and hope to many. Because of the miraculous healings that occurred night after night, the whole city was stirred and ten 'Bethel' churches were planted in North Staffordshire out of the highly-successful evangelistic campaigns.

Clearly such sketch portraits emphasise the role of Methodist-based Christian leaders and congregations more than that of other denominations. However, a survey of all Christian congregations and denominations in the area through history is beyond the scope of this book. And it was the Methodist approach to vital Christian faith which shaped the character of the area in its period of expansion and development.

Up and down

The early years of the 20th Century dawned bright for the Potteries towns. The 1920s was to prove a high point in terms of economic production and social progress, at the time the City was being granted its charter by King George V. At that point, 50% of the entire population was employed in the pottery industry, while thousands more laboured in the foundries and the numerous coal mines. From that decade onwards, however, just as a new chapter was dawning for the new city, the first hints of decline in steel production, coal mining and the pottery industry were being felt.

As the 20th Century progressed, the slump experienced during and after the Second World War proved pivotal. In the 1950s and 1960s, the decline in traditional manufacturing accelerated. It seemed that the writing was on the wall for the City of Stoke-on-Trent and its industries. The steel production, pottery and coal-mining which had been the colossal strength of the area were fast becoming its fatal weakness. The historically narrow focus that had enabled progress, honed skills and ensured success would now become a great hindrance, since diversification into new areas of business was a necessity.

This put Stoke-on-Trent at a great disadvantage in comparison to other comparable cities. Though they were facing similar challenges and changes, other cities had a more diverse base of industry, experience and skill. Stoke-on-Trent had almost no other skills and industries on which to fall back. Because of its unique geography and history, it also had no long heritage of academic education, no university, no cathedral and no historic city centre.

Lost cause?

Not only was there a growing realisation that the old was passing, but there was no real sense of the new that might be beckoning. Worse still, the industrial heritage had left behind huge and indelible blots on the landscape, as well as on the psyche of the people. Of course, general health, education and the standard of living were improving, but the city continued to fall behind other parts of the United Kingdom in many aspects of life – educational achievement, health, aspiration and wealth, to name but a few.

The collective mood of despair was, perhaps, best summed up by Richard Crossman, Minister of Housing in the Labour Government, when he visited Stoke-on-Trent in February 1965. The contents of his journal for that day are worth reporting in full. As he drove through the city, he came to the conclusion that the city was a lost cause, writing;

> Here is this huge, ghastly conurbation of five towns – what sense is there in talking about urban renewal here? Other towns have a shape, a centre, some place where renewal can start, perhaps a university. But if one spent billions on this ghastly collection of slag heaps, pools of water, old potteries, deserted coal mines, there would be nothing to show for the money.

> There is nothing in Stoke except the worst of the industrial revolution and some of the nicest people in the world. I felt even more strongly that it was impossible to revive Britain without letting such places as Stoke-on-Trent decline. Indeed, I began to wonder whether it was not really better to let it be evacuated; renewal is an impossibility, or alternatively a fantastic waste of money.[6]

These are remarkable sentiments indeed, coming from such a prominent government minister of the time. They are also telling as a perspective of city life which is based entirely on materialistic and utilitarian values, to the exclusion of the spiritual, social and cultural. Such negative responses to the challenges facing Stoke-on-Trent at that point might explain why there was a startling absence of inward investment into the area during the second half of the 20th Century, and even a semi-serious debate about whether to delete the city from

---

[6] Diary entry of Richard Crossman for Saturday 6 February 1965.

the map altogether. At least the local population was considered nice enough to allow them to be evacuated before the bombs were dropped on the city....

Attempts at renewal

The closing years of the 20th Century heralded a new period of investment into the city, however, with money coming from the European Union, national government, the Coalfields Regeneration Board and other regeneration bodies. Billions of pounds were spent and many good things were accomplished. However, in light of the vast number of houses, factories, pot-banks and slag-heaps to clear, coupled with the great amount of new infrastructure to build, the task was huge and progress proved slow.

It was in this context that the Experian report of September 2001 was published. While the local media were jumping to defend the city, my long-time friend and partner-in-Christian-work Lloyd Cooke and I sat down in our office suite in Burslem to talk over the findings of the Experian report and the response it had elicited within the city. Together we considered what a Christian response to the turn of events might look like. We could not have guessed at the outcome of our conversation of that afternoon in late September 2001.

2: THE MINISTRY OF DESPERATION

At a practical level, it was not difficult for Lloyd and me to hold a conversation about the Experian report. We met regularly to share together, to consider direction and plan events, because our offices were situated adjacent to each other in the same building in Moorland Road, Burslem, in the northern part of Stoke-on-Trent. Lloyd headed up The Saltbox Christian Resource Centre[1], while I led City Vision Ministries.

Inter-church agencies

The Saltbox had been established in 1983 by a group of local Methodists as a resource agency for Christian people, churches and organisations in Stoke-on-Trent and the surrounding area of North Staffordshire. Its first roles included the provision of stage props, books and cassette tapes for Christians to borrow. Lloyd joined the Saltbox as its director on 1 February 1988, having previously worked for two bastions of local society, the Michelin Tyre Company and the Sentinel newspaper. Under Lloyd's visionary leadership, the Saltbox had been transformed into a strategic and effective inter-church agency, providing information, building networks, liaising with the secular media and stimulating spiritual vision for the area.

---

[1] The Saltbox Christian Resource Centre was then more commonly known as The Saltbox Christian Centre. More recently, it has come to be known as The Saltbox.

After leading Assemblies of God congregations in Kent and Stoke-on-Trent, I had founded City Vision Ministries in March 1994 as an inter-denominational research, prayer, teaching and consultation ministry for churches in Stoke-on-Trent. Under the umbrella of City Vision Ministries, I had spent considerable time researching the city's past and present, gaining understanding about its heritage and culture, its present challenges and future aspirations. The information uncovered had been used to fan the flames of insight, vision and intercessory prayer for the area.

Complementary work

In addition to our different and varied local inter-church ministries, through the 1990s Lloyd and I worked with several other Christian groups regionally, nationally and internationally. Together we had been involved in the national and international church planting agenda through such agencies as Saturation Church Planting International, Challenge 2000 and Together in Mission. Lloyd had strong connections within Methodism locally and nationally, while I was serving as a director of the Assemblies of God World Mission department and as a visiting lecturer in theology at the International Bible Training Institute in West Sussex.

Lloyd and I had first worked together in the summer of 1987, when he had taken the lead in organising a local version of the then-popular 'March for Jesus' praise marches in Stoke-on-Trent. The outcome was that 1,500 Christians had marched to and through the city centre on the afternoon of Saturday 19 September 1987. Our working relationship had been cemented the following year, when we organised and led 'Mission 88,' an inter-church mission week with well-known vicar Colin Urquhart and a further week of outreach using the 'King's Coaches' with Urquhart's fellow-leader Bob Gordon.

Through the 1990s, Lloyd and I had spearheaded many aspects and types of inter-denominational Christian expression in North Staffordshire. These included midweek gatherings addressed by nationally-known speakers and regular Christian leaders' meetings. We also ran monthly prayer breakfasts, which were held in a different venue on each occasion and which encouraged united prayer for the city and surrounding areas. Alongside these events, the Saltbox was busy collating and distributing information to local Christians and representing the church to the City Council and secular media. City Vision was informing, encouraging and supporting intercessors in and beyond the city limits. Undergirding all of this work was the respect and friendship between us, upon which our co-operative and complementary ministry was built.

Strong foundations

The 14 years of co-operation before 2001 was to stand Lloyd and I in good stead in what was to follow. In truth, nothing that the Lord does is done without the prior slow-and-steady work of foundation-laying. Human experience and Biblical testimony conspire to assure us that foundations are of the greatest possible importance. No building can stand the combined tests of time, wind and storm unless it has solid foundations. And the bigger the building, the deeper the foundations must go. All of us have witnessed the seemingly endless time taken by developers to clear a site and to work on the utilities and foundations before there is anything to show above ground for the investment and effort. And then, almost overnight, the building is speedily erected, once the foundations have been made secure.

If the process of building a house, for example, were to be laid out on a time-chart, the time taken to erect the walls and roof would be only a small fraction of the time taken in conceiving and developing the vision, drawing the detailed plans, obtaining planning consent, hiring contractors, clearing the site, providing utilities and laying the foundations. Similarly, in God's work in the world, any and all of God's apparently sudden interventions can be shown to have been preceded by long periods of preparation. The sudden and dramatic impact of the miracle, the healing or the prophecy comes only because most of the people who witness it were not aware of the unseen preparations taking place. For those who see and know, however, and who were involved in the hidden work of vision-birthing and foundation-laying, the breakthrough may be sudden, but it is certainly neither unknown nor unexpected.

In Stoke-on-Trent in 2001, the breakthrough we were to experience in city-focused prayer apparently emerged from nowhere, but its roots and foundations lay in the many hours given sacrificially by lone intercessors and by small, unheralded gatherings of Christians on their knees in prayer to God on behalf of the city and its churches. Such small groups and networks exist in every area of the country and all future success of the Gospel in the nation depends on their vital service to God. The church, and the nation, owes a great debt to such selfless intercessors.

Inspirational example
I am not suggesting that the foundations of God's work in Stoke-on-Trent date back only to the work done by Lloyd, myself and others from 1987 onwards, of course. We were certainly not the first to hold the city and its churches in our hearts. We were very much aware of the foundation laid, for example, by Rev. Bob Dunnett, a well-known Christian leader, who for many years lectured at Birmingham Bible College[2] and who led the regional 'Pray for Birmingham' and national 'Pray for Revival' movements.

---

[2] It is now called Birmingham Christian College.

Prior to his work in Birmingham, Bob and his wife Mary (always known as Di) served as a Church of England curate from early 1961 to late 1972 in one of the most deprived areas of Stoke-on-Trent. During that time, Bob organised and led meetings to pray for revival in the parish of Bucknall-with-Bagnall in which he served. He also met with other church leaders to pray for revival. Many of these monthly meetings took place in Bethesda Chapel, the scene of large, impressive and sustained pulses of revival throughout the 19th Century.

It was while living and working in the Potteries that Bob was first involved in wider expressions of prayer for revival. These included the music-based event written by Americans Jimmy and Carol Owens entitled 'If my people...,' which was based on the promise of God in the Old Testament:

> ...if my people, who are called by my name, will humble themselves and pray and seek my face and turn from their wicked ways, then I will hear from heaven, and I will forgive their sin and will heal their land' (2 Chronicles 7:14).

Long before Bob was more widely known for his inspirational leadership of the national Pray for Revival movement, he was laying his own foundations in the ministry of prayer, while simultaneously re-digging foundations of prayer laid over centuries in North Staffordshire. Eternity alone will reveal the debt owed by the church and city for the visionary service of Bob and Di Dunnett.

Observable trend

For united prayer for the area had not begun with Bob Dunnett. The Christian story in North Staffordshire would be incomplete without reference to the place of passionate prayer among God's people down the centuries. For example, in early 1855 the young evangelist William Booth conducted seven weeks of outreach meetings in the area. Moving from Longton to Hanley, then to Burslem and the neighbouring market town of Newcastle-under-Lyme, Booth was impacted by the intensity of the spiritual fervour he witnessed among Potteries people. To his fiancée and soon-to-be bride Catherine Mumford, Booth wrote:

> The work progresses very favourably. Chapels crowded every night - riveted attention for an hour and a quarter's sermon and then mighty Prayer Meetings such as *you never saw*.[3]

Booth went on to note that the daily prayer meetings continued on until well after 10.00pm and sometimes ended not much before midnight. Not only were the prayer sessions lengthy, but they were also accompanied by loud cries and physical movements as the people engaged in heartfelt prayer to God for their own salvation, as well as that of others.

A generation earlier, the Primitive Methodist revival had emerged from a grass-roots prayer movement in the area. Converted coal-miners were so upset that the prayer meetings were not long enough to allow them all to have a turn at public prayer, they requested longer prayer meetings. In response, they were promised a whole day's praying at Mow Cop, a promise fulfilled on Sunday 31 May 1807, when more than 2,000 people gathered to spend the day in prayer at the summit of that historic, wind-swept hill. Based around this simple focus, that prayer meeting launched a world-impacting revival movement.

---

[3] Letter from William Booth to Catherine Mumford quoted in *Life of William Booth* by Harold Begbie, published by MacMillan and Co., London, 1926, pages 195-196. Capital letters and italics as Booth wrote them.

Such repeated references to the quality and power of prayer should not come as a surprise, considering the roots of Christianity into the area in the late seventh Century through St Chad and/or his followers. St Chad had travelled to the North Midlands from the Island of Lindisfarne.[4] Above all, the Celtic Christian Church, a movement which had converted the British Isles to the Christian faith from the fifth Century onwards, was known for the centrality and the intensity of its prayer-life.

The rule of life of the Celtic Christians was, 'Let everyone remain in or near his cell (personal room), waiting upon God in prayer, unless otherwise employed by the Holy Spirit.' If, as is likely, this community rule was followed by the earliest Christians meeting by the River Trent in Stoke, at the place now known as Stoke Minster, then the very foundation of the Christian heritage in the area was one of commitment to God in prayer. Upon this has been built the development and success of generations of faithful and committed Christian people.

Rock bottom

Now, however, as Lloyd and I talked together in late September 2001, for all the rich heritage and experience of Christian people in bygone generations, we had reached a point of desperation. It felt as though the city had reached rock bottom, with no lower to sink, no place to hide and no excuses to offer. We knew that the picture painted by the Experian report was generally and evidently accurate. In fact, we knew that the reality of the situation was, if anything, worse than the report indicated.

---

[4] Lindisfarne is also known as Holy Island on account of the holiness, spirituality and hospitality of the Celtic Christians who made their base there.

This was because two areas within our knowledge-base were not covered by the Experian report – politics and faith. In political terms, Stoke-on-Trent had been a Labour Party voting area through almost the entire 20th Century. As the 21st Century now dawned, however, there was wide-spread acknowledgement that such one-sided party politics had led to stagnation. While well-meaning, committed men and women still gave their time and energy to helping local residents, visionary leadership in and for the city seemed sadly lacking.

From a faith perspective, attendance at the 150 Christian congregations in the city had experienced steady decline throughout the 20th Century. Every indicator pointed to a bleak future for many of these congregations unless something changed radically. This had become clear to me in the mid-1990s, when I had undertaken research among churches of all denominations in several areas of the city. After writing about the state of churches in Hartshill and Trent Vale in 1997, I presented a report to the Bishop of Stafford entitled, 'The end of church as we know it.'

Therefore, Lloyd and I were as aware as anyone, and more aware than most, that we had indeed reached rock bottom in the city. It was a serious and challenging situation. What to think? What to say? What to do? By the grace of God, through our conversation that day the depth of desperation was transformed into an avenue of grace. We proved again the truth of the oft-repeated maxim, 'Man's extremity is God's opportunity.'[5]

Suddenly we understood. We were not to respond to the Experian report from the perspective of pride in our heritage or confidence in our ability to sort it out. Nor would we react

[5] The saying is attributed to Presbyterian preacher John Flavel (1627-1691).

by pointing accusing fingers in the direction of politicians, civil servants or business leaders, whether local or national. Rather it was time to humble ourselves, admit our need, seek the Lord in prayer and turn away from our sins.

Humility, prayer and repentance

This led us back to the Biblical text which Bob Dunnett and others had highlighted in the 1970s:

> ...if my people, who are called by my name, will humble themselves and pray and seek my face and turn from their wicked ways, then I will hear from heaven, and I will forgive their sin and will heal their land' (2 Chronicles 7:14).

This Old Testament text was set at the time of the dedication of the newly-built Jewish temple in Jerusalem. When King Solomon prayed for the presence and glory of God to fill the temple, the glory of God descended and priests and people were unable to stand in the face of God's splendour. Soon afterwards, the Lord appeared to Solomon, confirming that his prayers had been heard. The Lord then promised Solomon that if the people of Israel sinned at any time, causing the Lord to bring judgement on the people and the land, the humility, prayer and repentance of God's people would lead to divine forgiveness and the healing of the land.

Several principles are clear in this Bible verse. Firstly, the words 'the land' refer not only to the actual soil, but to the food which comes from it and to the quality of life that results from successful harvests and abundance of provision. In modern terms, 'the land' might, therefore, be understood as the provision of food, the proper use of the environment, the success of business, and the order, peace and vitality of society.

Secondly, God's people sometimes stray into sin and disobedience, and this sin has a negative impact on the land.

The whole of life - spiritual, social, political and economic - is adversely affected by disobedience to God's laws. Thirdly, forgiveness and healing requires humility of heart and mind, prayer, seeking God's face and repentance from sin. Repentance means to leave behind the attitude and act of rebellion and disobedience against God, to turn around 180 degrees to face God and to follow his ways once more.

Healing and transformation

Fourthly, when God's people turn back to him in this way, he graciously hears, forgives sin and heals the land. Forgiveness may begin in the human spirit, but it leads to blessing and healing on the individual, the church and on life in general. Forgiveness and the healing of God's people leads to renewal in economy, productivity in business, abundance of harvest and blessing on society. This is what is meant by the healing of the land.

By divine coincidence, in the summer 2001 a new series of videos was being distributed from Seattle, Washington. Entitled *Transformations*, each video contained the story of four or five places around the world where the united humility, prayer and repentance of the churches had led to exactly these spiritual, economic and social blessings. From India to Latin America, from Pacific Ocean islands to Africa, cities and regions were being transformed by God's power in answer to prayer and repentance. Lloyd had planned to show the first Transformations video at the Queen's Theatre, Burslem, in mid-October 2001. At the end of the event, he announced that a prayer meeting for the area would be held on the evening of Wednesday 31 October 2001 at the Bethel Christian Centre,[6] Abbey Hulton.

---

[6] Bethel Christian Centre had been known by various names over the years, but this was its name during the majority of the

Although schooled in the importance of good publicity through his previous role at the Sentinel newspaper, and despite still using promotional letters and posters for events on a regular basis, Lloyd did not feel that this repentance-prayer meeting should be widely promoted. His reasons for this included the shortness of time between the screening of the Transformations video and the proposed prayer meeting, the conviction that the Lord would draw people to the meeting and that 'to invite people to their own funeral' was not quite the thing to do!

Avenue of grace

On the morning of 31 October 2001 we brought together 25 Christian leaders from North Staffordshire at Shallowford House for a morning of reflection and prayer.[7] At this event, I gave a summary of the history of Stoke-on-Trent over two millennia, concluding the presentation with pointers to the desperate current situation, as illustrated by the findings of the Experian report. The group of leaders responded in prayer for God's mercy on the area. So, although it was Hallowe'en, our focus was not on battling with evil spiritual powers, but on humbling ourselves before the living God and seeking his mercy, forgiveness and healing.

Notwithstanding the lack of publicity for the event, around 200 people turned up at the Bethel Christian Centre that evening, representing several churches from across the area. More importantly, in the words of Lloyd, 'God showed up' as the people began to pray. Many people got down on

---

time in which the city-focused prayer meetings were held there. In the last three years it has been renamed Bethel City Church and is now called Breathe City Church.

[7] Shallowford House is the Lichfield Diocesan Conference Centre, situated

their hands and knees, while others lay prostrate on the floor, in response to the weight of God's presence. In view of such divine intervention, Lloyd consulted worship leader Paul Critchley, plus others present at the meeting, about how to take this forward.[8] In the words of Paul Critchley,

> Lloyd came over to me at the keyboard and asked if I knew what the date was for the last Wednesday in November. That established, he proceeded to the microphone announcing the next meeting just like it had been smoothly planned. I think that was the birthing moment for the new prayer movement.[9]

In this way, the moment of desperation opened an avenue of grace, for when we realise our helplessness and hopelessness in the face of overwhelming need, there the Lord steps in with his supply of unlimited favour and kindness to accomplish what we never could have achieved without him.

---

near Eccleshall, 15 miles south-west of Stoke-on-Trent.

[8] I was absent from the meeting, having travelled from Shallowford House to Dagenham during the afternoon of 31 October, in order to fulfil a long-standing commitment to address a gathering of church leaders belonging to the London Region of Assemblies of God.

[9] E-mail from Paul Critchley, 21 July 2011.

3: DEEPER, MUCH DEEPER

Following the powerful repentance-prayer meetings of 31 October 2001, two more '2 Chronicles 7:14' prayer meetings were held on Friday 30 November. The first of these saw church leaders gather at the Bethel Christian Centre for a morning of worship, prayer and repentance, concluding with a simple buffet lunch. Once more the presence of God hovered over the meeting, as leaders were invited to take off the defence mechanisms of their leadership role, position and title, and to come together to the Lord first and foremost as followers of Jesus.

Protective clothing

The way in which the structure of the Christian church in this country developed means that Christian leaders and workers face a special challenge in the arena of public worship and prayer. For leaders are simultaneously followers of Jesus, members of a local church congregation and leaders of God's people. Their leadership role often implies a distinction of relationship and difference of function from the members of the congregation, especially during public church services. While most people attending a service are able to receive, to learn and to participate in specific ways, the church leader is usually 'working' as the meeting leader, preacher or celebrant of Holy Communion.

The church leader's approach to public meetings, therefore, is very different from that of the majority of church members. Yet while the function of the leaders of a

Christian meeting or congregation may be distinct from that of other congregational members, it is too easy for the leadership role to become a protective barrier behind which a leader hides. The 'professional' aspect of the work can overshadow the personal spiritual response of the leader. The city-wide corporate prayer meetings provided the opportunity for Christian leaders to participate in a meeting which they were not controlling, working or necessarily contributing publicly. This opportunity to 'come as a child of God rather than as a church leader' was often emphasised during the monthly leadership gatherings.

Thankfully, many leaders were able to relax and to receive from the Lord, even to the point of opening up and making themselves vulnerable among their brothers and sisters in Christ. Those who did so received significant release of spirit and found nothing other than support and encouragement from their fellow-leaders. Others struggled with the vulnerability of being in a profound spiritual environment among peers without the protective clothing of position, title and social standing behind which to hide.

Hot and cold

The deep work of the Holy Spirit among the church leaders at their meeting continued into the evening prayer meeting, when about 400 people gathered to worship and pray. Two hours passed as though a brief moment in the awe-inspiring presence of God, who was at work among his people, stirring hearts, renewing love for him, challenging wrong attitudes and behaviours and lifting vision to the wider community and its needs.

At the conclusion of the evening prayer meeting, it was decided to hold another prayer event at the end of December. Sunday 30 December was the chosen date, since a meeting on New Year's Eve might exclude those who had already committed to see in the New Year with family and friends. In view of normal Sunday morning local church commitments, 50 church leaders met instead at 4.30pm on Sunday 30 December for a time of sharing, testimony and prayer.

Privately Lloyd and I were concerned that not many people would venture out on a dark Sunday evening in the middle of the Christmas/New Year festive period. To add to our concerns, the weather proved to be extremely cold that day, with temperatures well below freezing and sheets of ice already on the ground by early evening. Would many people be willing to come out on such a frosty, midwinter night? Yet as we prayed prior to the public meeting in the upstairs room that looked out over the entrance and car park of the Bethel Christian Centre, we were amazed to see scores of cars and hundreds of people arriving well in advance of the starting time.

At that moment, it dawned upon us that we were being caught up in a something very significant, in which personal inconvenience and terrible weather were not sufficiently strong to deter people from participation. God was on the move. More than 500 people met together that evening for the third opportunity to humble ourselves, to seek the Lord in prayer and to repent from sin, so that the land might be healed. Over 30 congregations across North Staffordshire were represented in the meeting, from a variety of backgrounds. The main denominations represented were Anglican, Methodist and Charismatic/Pentecostal. The age range ran from children to the elderly. The worship was powerful, the prayer humbling, the common purpose stirring and the friendship heart-warming.

A name and a blessing

Mid-January 2002 witnessed the first use of the condensed title '2C7' to describe the new prayer movement, as opposed to the original '2 Chronicles 7:14' descriptor. Without objection or delay, the prayer-and-repentance movement became universally referred to as 'the 2C7 movement' or simply as '2C7.' This proved to be as defining and durable a name as it is simple and succinct. Also quickly initiated was the new parting blessing to be shared at the conclusion of each of the now-monthly prayer meetings. Every member of the congregation in every meeting was invited to shake a few people by the hand and/or to hug their friends, while speaking over each other the words, 'Deeper, much deeper.'

This specific and precise form of parting blessing was adopted out of the strong conviction that the Lord was digging deeper in our personal lives as we were digging deeper in prayer into the foundations of God's vision for the City of Stoke-on-Trent and its environs. While our hoped-for outcome was the healing of the land, the mode of progress in that direction was the deep, inner work of the Holy Spirit in the hearts of God's people. If we were to scale higher and reach wider, we had first to dig deeper.

Heart of the matter
This spiritual reality has a strong base in the Scriptures, where the innermost part of a human being is referred to as 'the heart.' Just as the physical heart lies at the core and centre of the working of the human body, so the spiritual heart is central to the life and well-being of the soul and personality. And although the soul and spirit are less tangible than the physical parts of the human anatomy, they are nonetheless real and vital to human life.

Thus almost 750 Bible verses are devoted to the importance of the heart. We are called to love the Lord with all our heart (For example, in Deuteronomy 6:5 and Mark 12:30, 33). This requires us to seek the Lord with all our heart (2 Chronicles 15:12, Psalm 84:2, Psalm 119:2). The

Lord promises that he will be found by all who do seek him wholeheartedly (Deuteronomy 4:29, Jeremiah 29:13). We are then to serve the Lord with heart and soul (Joshua 22:5, 1 Samuel 12:20, Colossians 3:23).

Since the condition of the heart is so important, we are to guard our heart (Proverbs 4:23), even as the Lord tests it for integrity and loyalty (1 Chronicles 29:17-18, Psalm 139:23). For it is easy for the heart to be distracted, corrupted and hardened (As with the Egyptian Pharaoh in Exodus 8:15, 19, 32; 9:34-35 and Israel's King Solomon in 1 Kings 11:4). In fact, the heart has a very real tendency to corruption (Matthew 15:19), wickedness (Genesis 6:5) and self-deception (Jeremiah 17:9).

The only remedy is to turn away from evil and to return to God with all our hearts (Joel 2:13). As we ask the Lord create a clean heart (Psalm 51:10), the Lord promises to give us a new heart and spirit within us (Ezekiel 11:19). Blessed with a new and pure heart, we can see God (Matthew 5:8), so long as we keep our heart focused (Psalm 86:11) and humble (Matthew 11:29). This is the path to deep-rooted joy (Psalm 4:7, Psalm 13:5) and well-being (Proverbs 3:5-8).

Dark cave of division

The 2C7 prayer gatherings of Thursday 31 January 2002 were once more remarkable for the numbers of church leaders and congregational members in attendance and for the deep work of the Spirit in our hearts. I addressed the meetings on the subject of 'the dark cave of division,' reflecting on the tragedy, from heaven's perspective, of division between Christian denominations, within denominations, between local churches and within local churches.

Dividing factors include doctrinal disputes (consubstantiation or transubstantiation, infant or believers' baptism, a-millennial or pre-millennial return of Jesus?), disagreement over worship style (hymns or choruses, organ or guitar?) and differences in leadership structure (priest or pastor, appointed elders or elected representatives?). Beside these issues of belief, structure and style, personal prejudice and the breakdown of personal relationships can arise. Not to mention disagreements over the thorny subject of finance...

The truth is that we Christian people have often made a mess of outliving the unity that is theirs by specific design and desire of God. Jesus prayed specifically for his followers –including those who would through the generations follow the original followers - that they would be one in the same way that Father, Son and Holy Spirit are one within the mystery of the trinity. As the Lord Jesus enunciated so clearly in his High Priestly prayer, such unity would not fail to cause the world to believe that Jesus had been sent from God (John 17:20-23). Such is the power of unity in Christ.

Unity in diversity

The challenge comes in understanding the nature of this unity and how it can be worked out in practice. We have to accept that historical, legal, cultural and financial legacies are almost impossible to put aside and that there will never be just one all-embracing denominational gathering of Christian people. And such a humanly-organised institution is neither desirable nor necessary, even if it were possible. For the goal of unity is not uniformity of thought, style and behaviour. Rather, the aim is unity of heart, of spirit, of attitude and of relationship, which has to be worked out within the context of diversity. Indeed, the greater the levels and degrees of diversity, the greater the miracle of unity lived out in practice. Unity arises from humility, respect and love, not from dictated behaviour or controlled environment.

Rev. Dr. Russ Parker, leader of the Acorn Christian Healing Foundation, was present at a 2C7 leaders' prayer meeting in early 2002. He noted the progress being made in the area of humility and mutual encouragement:

> What impressed me was the corporate desire to see transformation in the communities of the five towns. A whole variety of church traditions were represented but it was the commitment to mutual honouring and encouragement that stood out for me. What greatly enhanced this process was the honesty in which some contributors owned their church's history of petty rivalries which had divided their common purpose in serving the needs of their societies. There was a fresh wind blowing of confession and passion to work alongside each other.[1]

Unity does not begin with contract, organisation and institution. It begins with heart, with intention, with relationship, with humility and with repentance.

Humility and repentance

Following the presentation about division and disunity made at the evening prayer gathering of 31 January 2002, the 600 people present were invited to stand in turn in their denominational groupings and to read out a corporate statement of repentance on behalf of their denomination for wrong attitudes, words and actions against other Christian people, groups and denominations. As each group stood in turn to confess, hearts were melted across the room, both among those repenting and those receiving the apology. Surely heaven rejoiced that day as prejudices were removed, attitudes softened, narrow-mindedness banished and critical spirits rejected.

The new dawn was sealed as, for the first and only time in the seven-year history of 2C7, we broke bread together,

---

[1] E-mail from Russ Parker, 7 March 2011.

DANIEL 9:4-5

"I prayed to the Lord my God and confessed:
O Lord, the great and awesome God, who keeps his covenant of love with
all who love him and obey his commands, we have sinned and done
wrong. We have been wicked and have rebelled; we have turned away
from your commands and laws."

Statement of Repentance

"As a company of xxxxxxxxx *(Anglicans, Baptists, Catholics, etc)* we earnestly desire to openly confess both to one another and to the body of Christ, the sin of division and lack of unity within the churches across our region.

WE ACKNOWLEDGE our need of repentance in order to bring healing and restoration.

WE REPENT of any wrong attitudes, suspicion, harsh words and unloving deeds that have caused division within the Body of Christ across our region.

WE REPENT of our lack of desire to build deep relationships and lasting unity in the Body of Christ.

WE REPENT of our lack of purpose and passion to bring the gospel of Christ to the citizens of North Staffordshire.

WE HUMBLE ourselves before one another, asking forgiveness from God and our fellow Christians, and praying for grace to pursue those things that make for peace and unity. Amen."

no mean feat in itself with so many present and no routines or structures in place. Vicars and pastors administered the bread and wine as God's people demonstrated in as clear as a way as possible that, though there may be many congregations, there is only one church in the City of Stoke-on-Trent, which is the sum total of all those belong to the family of God by repentance, faith and baptism.

Cross Rhythms

The evening prayer gathering of 28 February 2002 was the only 2C7 prayer meeting not to be held at the Bethel Christian Centre. The venue on that occasion was Longton Central Hall, a large 19th Century Methodist building in the south of the city. With a large upstairs gallery, the building could seat 600 people – and it was mostly full for the 2C7 meeting that evening. The prayer gathering was special, not only for the different venue and the large numbers present, but also because, during the meeting, Cross Rhythms City Radio was launched.

Cross Rhythms is a Christian ministry founded by Chris and Kerry Cole in Plymouth in the 1980s, whose means of outreach work has been radio programmes, alongside music-based weekend camps and a rehabilitation centre for people with life-controlling addictions. The Coles moved from Plymouth to Stoke-on-Trent at the end of the 1990s and worked for a while with United Christian Broadcasters, another Christian media ministry based in the city. Now, however, Cross Rhythms was to launch its own specific City Radio ministry, aiming to engage with young people through culturally-relevant music programming.

In October 2001 (which is more than interesting from the perspective of timing), Cross Rhythms had been granted the UK's first one-year Community Access Radio license. The station had purchased the newly-redundant BBC Radio

Stoke premises in the City Centre and was ready to launch. In the context of the vibrant worship and united prayer of a congregation of almost 600 people, Cross Rhythms went on air at precisely 9.00pm on Thursday 28 February 2002. Its launch was heralded by a huge cheer from members of the congregation. The Lord had granted the 2C7 prayer movement, itself just a newborn baby, the privilege of witnessing and facilitating the birth of a new era of Christian radio in the City, and of Community Access Radio in the UK.

Giant of idolatry

At both 2C7 gatherings held on 28 February, I addressed the people on the issue of idolatry. This subject was felt to be especially relevant to Longton, the venue for our evening meeting. For the town of Longton has been traditionally less open to the Christian Gospel than other parts of the city. This may have been due to the strong history of spiritism in the town. It seemed right, therefore, to use the visit to Longton to address the issue in the context of repentance from personal idolatry. It may sound strange to suggest that Christians might be also involved in idolatry, but, since idolatry is defined as anything that gets in the way of the worship of God, or which takes the place which rightly belongs to God, it is possible even for followers of Jesus to be guilty of idolatrous thoughts, behaviours and lifestyles.

This can be outworked in such things as the cult of personality, the worship of worship, the love of money, sexual immorality, self-centredness, self-advancement at the expense of others and coveting that which belongs to others. The way out of any and all such forms of idolatry is to be found in the words of 2 Chronicles 7:14, '… if my people … will humble themselves and pray and seek my face and turn from their wicked ways ….' We must in repentance dethrone what that taken the place of Jesus and once more enthrone him in our heart.

The 2C7 prayer meeting of 31 March 2002 fell on Easter Sunday. To celebrate the occasion, we returned to Bethel Christian Centre on the Sunday evening and held an extended four-hour-long prayer meeting, from 8.00pm to midnight. This Easter meeting was different in style, not just in length, to the previous five prayer meetings. The euphoria of the first few meetings was already subsiding. The 2C7 movement was taking on a shape, focus and commitment to prayer for the healing of Stoke-on-Trent and North Staffordshire that would allow it to continue in the medium- to long-term. The scene was being set to dig yet deeper and to extend far wider.

4: WIDER, MUCH WIDER

2002 was proving to be a year of change and blessing. Long-held prejudices were being dissolved and deeply-held misconceptions corrected. Love for God was being re-ignited and passion for the transformation of Stoke-on-Trent fanned into flame. Commitment to prayer was being strengthened and the call to humility deepened.

Deep and wide

And then, without fanfare or herald, we discovered that the path before us was widening even as we committed ourselves to dig deeper in prayer. In fact, the more we set time aside to meet with God, the more the doors of opportunity opened before our eyes. Without any striving, 'Deeper, much deeper' was leading to 'wider, much wider.' Not that the widening stream removed the necessity or the reality of a deepening experience of God. Quite the opposite. The two ran alongside each other, inextricably intertwined, feeding into one another and off each other.

Such a deep/wide relationship may sound strange, even paradoxical, because human experience tells us that if a stream is widening, it must also necessarily be becoming shallower as grows wider. What may seem paradoxical to us, however, is not necessarily so to God. The spiritual realities of the kingdom of God are very often very different to our own human perspective on things. In God's economy, it is possible for a stream to be simultaneously going deeper and flowing wider. The two are not mutually exclusive. The fact that they occur simultaneously is a pointer to the power of God at work.

River of life

This is pictured for us beautifully in Ezekiel 47:1-12, when the prophet Ezekiel is given a vision of God's temple in Jerusalem, out of which is trickling a small stream. As the stream flows along, however, it becomes by stages ankle-deep, knee-deep, waist-deep and then deep enough to swim in. As the river deepens, however, it is clear that it is also becoming wide enough to described as 'a river that no-one could cross' (Ezekiel 47:5).

And this is not the only unusual property of the river that flows from God's throne. 'The river of God' consists of life-giving water. The supernatural power of this water is demonstrated by the fact that when the fresh water meets salt water, the salt water is immediately desalinated and purified to become fresh water. Therefore, swarms of all kinds of fish and sea-creatures are able to live and thrive in the heaven-fresh, life-giving water.

Fishermen are not able to exhaust the supplies, due to the abundance and variety of the fish stocks. On the river-bank, fruit trees proliferate and flourish. Their fruit is remarkable in that it becomes ripe on a monthly basis. And the quality of the fruit does not suffer by reason of its large quantity. 'Their fruit will serve for food and their leaves for healing,' all because of 'the water from the sanctuary' of God's throne gives them life (Ezekiel 47:12).

Heaven and earth

So the life of heaven brought life to earth in the form of fish and figs, haddock and healing. Deep and wide, heaven and earth, vertical and horizontal merge in the kingdom of

God. This was our experience during 2002. Many of the prayer meetings that year were remarkable for the weight of the presence of God and for the way in which Christian leaders opened their hearts to the Lord and to each other within the context of that holy atmosphere.

The church leaders' prayer meeting of May 2002 was especially notable in that the basic programme was completely shelved, being overtaken by an extended time of worship and confession of sin as the Spirit of God swept across the meeting. One leader confessed to drinking too much wine as a means of escape from the pressures of life. Another leader admitted to a guilty conscience that their home was not kept as clean and tidy as it should be. Consciousness of time evaporated in the all-encompassing presence of God, as eternal matters overtook the earthly and mundane. Such times can be neither planned nor produced by human effort. All we can do is to bow the knee, humble the heart and respond to the revelation of the glory of God.

Political momentum

2002 was also notable for the connection of the prayer movement with political developments in the City of Stoke-on-Trent. Clearly Lloyd and I were not the only ones thinking that new vision, energy and momentum were required in the political life of the city. At the time, the government was proposing to several cities that they should consider moving away from the traditional electoral system, in which local councillors were elected ward by ward, with the largest political grouping on the council forming the ruling party.

The new options included the possibility of local voters electing a mayor directly, as well as choosing local councillors. Arrangements would then be put in place to stipulate how the elected mayor and the City Council would work together. Essentially, however, the elected mayor would have a significant influence over direction and policy. The purpose of the new system was to break free from the inherited prevalent party political stagnation and to stimulate forward movement.

Locally, the director of the Stoke-on-Trent Citizen's Advice Bureau, Mike Wolfe, decided to take advantage of this government initiative and began to lobby for the introduction of an 'elected mayor' system in the city. His 'Mayor4Stoke' campaign found support with many local business and social leaders, as well as favour with the Sentinel newspaper, which enthusiastically backed the idea. The campaign encountered opposition from other civic leaders, including the sitting councillors of all political persuasions.

Time for change

The first challenge for Mike Wolfe's campaign was to raise thousands of signatures requesting a ballot about the proposed new system. Interestingly, some would say amazingly, the requisite number of signatures was gathered. This triggered a mini-referendum on the issue of whether or not to adopt the elected mayoral system. The referendum was to be held alongside the normal annual election of one third of the city councillors on Thursday 2 May 2002.

Therefore, the 2C7 prayer meeting of the evening of Tuesday 30 April 2002 was to take place just two days in advance of the City Council elections and the referendum concerning whether to adopt the new 'elected mayor' system of local government. The timing of the two events in relation to each other provided a significant, God-given opportunity to pray together on 30 April for God's intervention into city life on 2 May.

We decided not only to pray for the political future of the city at the prayer meeting of 30 April, but also to invite five guests to speak for or against the proposed new mayoral system. The information provided was to stimulate thinking as well as to fuel prayer. On the evening of 30 April, over 500 Christians from across North Staffordshire gathered to listen to the invited speakers and to respond in prayer. Mike Wolfe, leader of the 'Mayor4Stoke' campaign, argued for the introduction of the new system, while representatives of the three main political parties argued for the retention of the existing system. Following the presentations, a time of focused intercessory prayer for the forthcoming election and referendum ensued.

New day

Two days later, the citizens of Stoke-on-Trent were presented with completely unexpected results from the City Council election and the referendum. The 'Mayor4Stoke' campaign had secured a 58% vote in favour of the change to the new elected mayoral system. And, for only the second time since 1945, the Labour Party had lost political control of Stoke-on-Trent, losing council seats across the city, including those of the council leader and the deputy leader.

It was a defining day in the political history of Stoke-on-Trent. Though a disastrous day for the local Labour Party, the significance to us seemed to lie in the end of an era and the dawn of a new day, mirroring in the political world what the Lord was doing with us in the spiritual realm. The 2C7 movement was neither in favour of, nor against, any mainstream political party *per se*. Nor did it ever campaign for one political party as opposed to another. However, we were, I believe, walking through a new door that the Lord was opening, and whenever the Lord opens a door, it becomes unshuttable (Revelation 3:7). The important thing is to be aware of what the Lord is doing and to follow him through the door of opportunity.

Once the referendum had determined that a new system would be introduced, the big question quickly switched to who the elected mayor would be. Eventually 12 people declared themselves as candidates for the role and began to present their credentials for the job. Once more the local media was heavily involved in keeping the public informed with the election news. Not only was the fact that the city was voting for an elected mayor new and different, but even the manner of voting was new and experimental. It was to be an all-postal ballot, with voting papers distributed at the beginning of October 2002. The last date for the return of ballot papers was Thursday 17 October.

Elected mayor
It seemed right to hold another special 'elected mayor' focused prayer event for the city under the banner of 2C7, so a prayer meeting was arranged to take place on Monday evening 7 October 2002. All 12 mayoral candidates were invited to attend and to speak for four minutes each on the subject 'Why I would make the best elected mayor of Stoke-on-Trent.'

Eleven of the 12 candidates accepted the invitation to attend and speak, the British National Party representative being the only one to decline. Once more the prayer meeting was packed with hundreds of Christians and, once more, the event was a resounding success. As a result of the presentations made, hearts and minds were influenced and directed. As a result of the prayers offered, heaven was touched and the city changed.

The mayoral election count and result could not have been more gripping. One major element of the equation was the high vote for the BNP, whose candidate polled 18.67% of the total vote. The two front-runners were George Stevenson, veteran Labour Party Member of Parliament for Stoke South Constituency, and Mike Wolfe, former Labour Party member and now independent candidate.

Stevenson had the edge after the first round of voting, but, under the voting system adopted, the second votes of those eliminated in the first rounds of counting were added to the candidates remaining in the race. This meant that, after the final re-allocation of votes, Mike Wolfe had pipped George Stevenson to the post by just over one half of one per cent. A new day had truly dawned. A new mayoral system had been introduced. A new mayor had been elected. And the 2C7 prayer movement had played a part, both publicly and behind the scenes, in what the Lord was doing.

'Samaritan' ministries
Another very different area of influence into the city that began to open up in 2002 we named 'Samaritan ministries' after the 'Good Samaritan' of Biblical fame.[1] It was this unnamed Samaritan who, in the parable of Jesus, offered medical, practical and financial help to a victim of mugging, even though the victim came from an ethnic background different from, and hostile to, his own. The modern outworking of this principle came in the form of financial aid and practical support for two Christians working among asylum seekers and refugees, who were at the time beginning to arrive in Stoke-on-Trent in considerable numbers.

Until the early 2000s, ethnic minority immigration into the city had been surprisingly low in numerical terms.[2] Most of the immigrants into the city in the post-war years had been of Pakistani origin. Now, however, Africans and Asians were arriving from various nations in increasing numbers, to be followed by Eastern Europeans as the decade progressed. Thankfully, some traditionally British churches

---

[1] The story can be found in Luke 10:29-37.

[2] 3.1% of the city's population belonged to ethnic minority groups according to the 1991 Census.

2C7: NORTH STAFFS 2001-2004

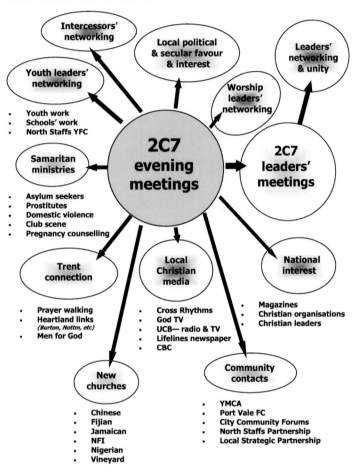

Intercessors' networking

Local political & secular favour & interest

Leaders' networking & unity

Youth leaders' networking

Worship leaders' networking

- Youth work
- Schools' work
- North Staffs YFC

2C7 evening meetings

2C7 leaders' meetings

Samaritan ministries

- Asylum seekers
- Prostitutes
- Domestic violence
- Club scene
- Pregnancy counselling

Trent connection

Local Christian media

National interest

- Prayer walking
- Heartland links
  (Burton, Nottm, etc)
- Men for God

- Cross Rhythms
- God TV
- UCB— radio & TV
- Lifelines newspaper
- CBC

- Magazines
- Christian organisations
- Christian leaders

New churches

- Chinese
- Fijian
- Jamaican
- NFI
- Nigerian
- Vineyard

Community contacts

- YMCA
- Port Vale FC
- City Community Forums
- North Staffs Partnership
- Local Strategic Partnership

Publisher/2C7/2C7 Flow chart
1/9/04

were taking advantage of the opportunity and opening their doors in welcome and hospitality. Others were becoming even more intentional in offering food and clothing, as well as help with accommodation and legal applications and appeals. Foremost among them was Peter Hulme, leader of Burslem Elim Church. It was a privilege to help Peter with financial gifts towards the hire of a minibus for use in his work among needy refugees.

Another aspect of practical outreach work was being undertaken by Brian and Janet Street, together with Margaret Donellan. They were going out onto the streets in the city on a regular basis to offer food, support and prayer for the city's prostitutes. We were able to provide some financial support to enable their work among the needy women to continue and develop.

A different kind of practical Christian care was developed and led by Dawn Reynolds (later Deaville). Dawn had always been gifted in communicating with people on the fringes of society, and she targetted the poor and needy, homeless and destitute for her 'VIP' events. Dawn would ask local Christians for donations of clothes and beauty products for the purpose of blessing women who had nothing. She also asked local hairdressers and manicurists for the gift of an evening of their time. The material gifts and the gifts of time were then put together to create an evening event to which the needy could be invited and pampered as VIPs. The ladies would be given clothes and care products, and receive massages, haircuts and so on. In this way, the love of Christ was demonstrated in practical terms to those on the edges of society.

Trent Connection

The expanding vision and influence of the 2C7 prayer movement was now to begin to extend beyond the

The Trent Connection

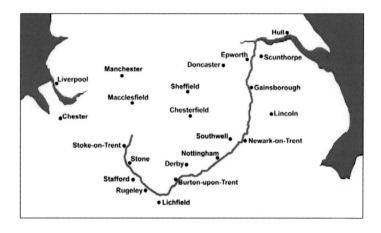

boundaries of Stoke-on-Trent. On 19 March 2002 Anne Donaldson, a member of the women's 'AGLOW' national board, wrote to Lloyd and me about a vision she had seen of the River Trent, which ran through the village where she lived, some ten miles downstream from Stoke-on-Trent. In the vision she had seen a bore-like wave of repentance running from Stoke-on-Trent to Stone and Burton-on-Trent, then on to Nottingham, Newark-on-Trent, Gainsborough and Hull. Anne saw the wave made up of many 'faceless' people, indicating that the character of the wave was of a spontaneous people movement, rather than a human-based personality cult. There were many tributaries flowing into and expanding the river as it went. There was also much debris brought to the surface from the churning of the water.

Lloyd and I both took the vision on board. Within a short time it began to bear fruit in several ways. At the extended prayer meeting on Easter Sunday 2002, prayer for blessing to flow along the path of the River Trent was one of the six areas of prayer undertaken. Then in April and May 2002, I presented a historical and strategic overview of the river, in which I focused on its importance as a barrier, a highway, a trade route, a source of power, the birthplace of revivalists and a historic conduit for revival. This led to prayer that the Lord would flow up and down the river to the villages, towns and cities on the way, reviving his work in the strategic Trent Valley.

Prayer walking

Through the summer, Lloyd took this very much to heart and conceived a plan to prayer-walk the route of the Trent from its source at Biddulph Moor, just to the north of Stoke-on-Trent, to Burton-on-Trent, some 30 miles to the south-east. The idea was that, since we longed for God to bless us, we should deliberately invest time and energy in praying for others. In the words of the Lord Jesus, 'Give and it will be given to you...' (Luke 6:38).

Therefore, on 5 September 2002, a group of seven 2C7 core leaders wrote a letter to the church leaders in Burton informing them of the plan to walk from Stoke to Burton over a two-day period. Lloyd would lead the walk and would be joined by three or four men on the journey. This walk took place in the autumn of 2002 and concluded with a prayer meeting of the walkers and some Christian leaders from Burton-on-Trent. It was at this meeting that some of the Burton leaders raised the idea of walking down the path of the River Trent from Burton-on-Trent to Nottingham, to which the Stoke-based prayer-walkers intuitively responded by saying that they would join in!

Lloyd and a few local prayer-walkers eventually walked from Stoke-on-Trent to Burton, from Burton to Nottingham, from Nottingham to Newark-on-Trent, from Newark-on-Trent to Gainsborough and from Gainsborough to the Humber, in five separate stages, each stage lasting two or three days. The first walk had been undertaken in autumn 2002 and the last leg was completed by four walkers in July 2004.

The prayer-walking story did not end there, however. Once the length of the River Trent had been successfully walked, Lloyd felt it right to walk north-west from Stoke-on-Trent, following the line of the Trent and Mersey Canal to the River Mersey near Liverpool. This 45-mile-long route had been vitally important to the development of the Potteries in the 18th Century, allowing finished ware to be transported quickly, directly, safely and in large quantities to the port of Liverpool, from where it could be transported by ship to Ireland and the Americas. This prayer walk was completed over three days from 20-22 October 2004.

Once the walk to Liverpool had been accomplished, Lloyd then decided to walk due north to Carlisle, a distance of some 150 miles. This walk was completed in a series of 10-15 miles segments during the year 2005, through sun and rain, cold and heat – and always accompanied by sore feet. The vision and blessing being received in Stoke-on-Trent was beginning once more to extend to the national arena.

Discerning strategy
Thus in various ways the prayer journey that was taking us deeper into the heart of God was also opening doors and spreading wider into the city and beyond. A strategy was becoming evident, though not a strategy that was being conceived and developed by brilliant brain-work or dynamic discussion. Rather, it was becoming clear by looking backwards and thus piecing together how the Lord was at work in all that was developing.

Perhaps we should not have been surprised to observe how perfectly the various strands of strategy fitted together and led us along a path to propel us forwards into the fulness of the purpose of God. At that point Lloyd and I took the conscious decision to continue in prayer, to trust God for the discernment of his heart and his plan, and to resist the temptation to sit down and draw up programmes and plans for the next stages of the journey. We simply wanted to follow the Lord into all the depth and scope that he purposed for us. By his grace, that is what happened.

5: INTIMACY, HUMILITY AND UNITY

2003 saw the continuation and development of our 2C7 journey, as we built upon the foundations laid in the first 15 months of repentance and prayer. Christian leaders attended the prayer events in consistent numbers, the last Monday of the month now becoming the regular set meeting time for such meetings. Two hundred people still attended the evening prayer meetings, now regularly held on the last Wednesday of each month, excluding the months of August and December.

The prayer movement inevitably could not continue to scale the heights of excitement experienced in the first few months, but it did manage to transition into a mature group of highly committed people from different churches and organisations who were serious about preparing the way for the healing of the land.

Valuing values

Although none of us wanted to get in the Lord's way by writing a strategy plan for the future, neither did we want the 2C7 prayer movement to lack clear foundations. Therefore Lloyd and I decided to try to capture the character of the unfolding prayer journey by writing a set of values. By doing so, we could track and describe the work of God as it developed, rather than trying to anticipate, and thereby influence, its future direction, size and scope.

Values are extremely important for any group, organisation or church, because they determine how the group's purpose and vision are to be pursued and fulfilled. Within the context of Christian faith, the ends do not automatically justify the means. How we conduct ourselves on the journey is just as important as our safe arrival at the final destination. Values are also useful in keeping us on track, providing a measure against which to test our progress, successes and challenges. A further use for a values statement lies in describing and defining the character of the group as a constant reminder for those who belong, as well as an introduction for those who join the journey at various stages along the way.

So in the Spring of 2003, after consultation with Lloyd and members of the 2C7 steering group, I attempted to capture on paper our defining characteristics and shared values. I came up with six simple sentences and presented them to the church leaders at the leaders' prayer meeting in late June 2003. Feedback was invited and received. Then, at a prayer retreat in early October, the six values were accepted as presented and a seventh value was added to address the issue of God's ability to work in surprising ways. The second draft became the final version, which was to act as a guide and point of reference for us on the journey between 2003 and 2008.

With the benefit of hindsight, I believe that we succeeded in accurately representing how the Lord was shaping and leading us from the early days of the 2C7 movement. Here, then, follows a description of the seven values, together with the thinking behind them and the way in which they related to the situation in Stoke-on-Trent.

Intimacy with God
Our first value was encapsulated in the sentence **'Intimacy with God is our first calling and priority.'** In line with the sentiment of this value, it was always put in first place in the list! We were very conscious that the primary calling

Glory of God

FOUNDATIONAL VALUES

1. Intimacy with God is our first calling and priority.

2. Humility, honesty and integrity are vital to the development of Christian character.

3. Meaningful relationships provide strength, support and accountability.

4. The kingdom of God impacts every area of personal and corporate life.

5. Leaders who empower all God's people are the key to the future.

6. Arrival at the destination demands commitment in the long term.

7. God often works outside the parameters of our understanding and experience.

of the new prayer movement was to come back to God. This calling preceded every other factor. True, we wanted to see the glory of God revealed in North Staffordshire, to experience the fires of revival, to know God's blessing and to be better people, but more than anything we were being called back to an intimate relationship with God.

Some might think it strange that the Lord needed to call his people back to himself, since it is very clear in the Bible that God should always occupy the first place. As the first of the Ten Commandments succinctly puts it, 'You shall have no other gods before me' (Exodus 20:3). This great commandment is echoed in the New Testament, where the first commandment is framed in the call of Jesus to 'Love the Lord your God with all your heart and with all your soul and with all your mind' (Matthew 22:37).

However, as the Bible describes and as human experience repeatedly demonstrates, it is all too easy to lose focus and to neglect the priority of knowing God. Our hearts are prone to lose their first love for God and to grow cold, as the Christians in Ephesus did almost 2,000 years ago (Revelation 2:4). The flames of passion require continual re-fuelling and fanning, if they are not to die away.

Common distractions

In practice, hearts become cold most often through the many distractions of daily life. Life is consumed with busyness, eaten up by commitment to family members, work, school, study, travel, house-work, shopping, sport, leisure, television, e-mail and the internet. It can too often seem too difficult to find time for regular spiritual devotions, even among devoted followers of Jesus. Many of these daily commitments are good and necessary, of course. This does not, however, negate the call and commandment to put God in first place. It does, of course, present us with a challenge about how to structure our lives in order to work out this priority in practice. It is impossible for anyone to impose a universal structure of life on others. Each of us has to work this priority out in our own lives in the fear of God (Philippians 2:12).

In some cases, the priority of love for God is lost for more sinister reasons, for example, through sinful thoughts, mind-sets and habits. The pull of human nature can lead us away from God, rather than towards him. From God's perspective, the only legitimate response to sin is to decisively turn away from it and to turn back to the living God. This is the issue, of course, which the call and promise of 2 Chronicles 7:14 directly addresses, namely, that when God's people have turned away from him in their hearts and by their behaviour, they will experience divine judgement. However, if they will return to the Lord with humility, prayer and repentance, the Lord will forgive, heal and restore.

Through the 2C7 movement, God's people were being drawn into a renewed, deeper and more intimate relationship with God the Father. For this reason God the Son laid down his life, so that we might come to the Father through him (John 14:6). Now God the Holy Spirit was doing his designated work of drawing God's people back to God the Father through God the Son (John 14:26).

Christ-like character

The second 2C7 value was **'Humility, honesty and integrity are vital to the development of Christian character.'** We cannot draw intimately close to God and remain unaffected in terms of attitude, behaviour and character. To know God, and to be known by him, is to undergo personal transformation. To claim to be close to God without displaying the evidence of a changed and changing character is unsustainable.

It is God's purpose to refine us and to make us more like Jesus as we love him, draw close to him and follow him. The journey to Christ-likeness is neither automatic nor guaranteed, however. It requires ongoing positive responses from us to co-operate with the Lord in his intention to make us like Jesus. The first step on this transformational journey is to realise the scale and depth of our own human failure in the face of a pure and holy God.

A perfect illustration of this journey is found in the experience of the Old Testament prophet Isaiah, who was confronted with a revelation of the living God. The sight was certainly awe-inspiring:

> In the year that King Uzziah died, I saw the Lord, high and exalted, seated on a throne; and the train of his robe filled the temple. Above him were seraphim, each with six wings: With two wings they covered their faces, with two they covered their feet, and with two they were flying. And they were calling to one another: 'Holy, holy, holy is the LORD Almighty; the whole earth is full of his glory.' At the sound of their voices the doorposts and thresholds shook and the temple was filled with smoke (Isaiah 6:1-4).

Humility and honesty

In the face of the holiness of God, Isaiah immediately and deeply sensed his own unworthiness, being in his own words 'ruined' by the majestic presence of God (Isaiah 6:5). As Isaiah called out in agony of spirit, one of the angelic seraphim touched his lips with a living coal from the altar and pronounced him clean from his sin and guilt (Isaiah 6:6-7). From this place of forgiveness and cleansing, he was able to answer the call to become a prophetic mouthpiece for God (Isaiah 6:8-13).

All God's people go through personal revelations of the living God, which, though they may not be as dramatic or startling as Isaiah's, are nevertheless real, deep and life-changing. The first such revelation marks the beginning of living Christian faith, while all subsequent revelations of God are mile-stones on the ongoing journey of faith. As each revelation of the glory of God is given, so the depth of sin is uncovered, the reach of divine grace is revealed and a new level of holiness received.

What cannot stand in the presence of God are pride, dishonesty and hypocrisy. To deny the reality and awfulness of sin is to lose the opportunity of divine forgiveness. To respond to the Lord in pride and dishonesty is to remove the opportunity to experience God's life-transforming power. To be humble and honest in God's presence, on the other hand, opens the way for the Lord to forgive, to heal, to transform and to re-energise with his divine power.

The challenge for God's people, therefore, is to maintain a humble spirit and an open, honest heart. The Lord requires truth in the innermost part of our lives. Therefore, pretence has no place in Christian character and relationships. And show, hype and exaggeration have no place in Christian meetings. The Lord is looking for humility, honesty and integrity.

Meaningful relationships

This leads us on to the third of the seven 2C7 values, which stated that **'Meaningful relationships provide strength, support and accountability.'** As we draw close to God and sense his transforming power in our character, we are inevitably drawn towards other Christian believers in meaningful relationship.

Christian faith may be forged in the depths of the human heart, but it is not meant to be lived out exclusively internally and personally. On the contrary, the context of Christian faith is always plural and corporate. Christian believers are described as fellow-citizens in a spiritual nation and members of a heavenly family (Ephesians 2:19), as living stones in a holy temple (1 Peter 2:5) and even as parts of a body (1 Corinthians 12:12-31). Each of these pictures suggests belonging, identity and purpose, yet above all they point to the non-negotiable strength of the relationship between each member in the nation, family, building and body.

The unity of the disciples of Jesus weighed heavily on the heart and mind of the Lord Jesus immediately prior to his death. In his high-priestly prayer on the night before he died, he prayed eloquently and sincerely for the unity of God's people in the following words:

My prayer is not for them alone. I pray also for those who will believe in me through their message, that all of them may be one, Father, just as you are in me and I am in you. May they also be in us so that the world may believe that you have sent me. I have given them the glory that you gave me, that they may be one as we are one — I in them and you in me — so that they may be brought to complete unity. Then the world will know that you sent me and have loved them even as you have loved me (John 17:20-23).

Understanding the nature of this Christ-like unity has exercised theologians over the last 2,000 years. How to work it out in reality is at least as challenging. Yet we cannot avoid the issue, as though the Lord did not pray this prayer. We are called to recognise that our lives are not our own. We belong to the Lord and, through him, to his people.

The power of unity

Sadly, Christian relationships are too often marked and marred by fear, pride and/or prejudice in one party, or both. Selfish ambition and hidden agendas are too often evident. Consequently we live in physical proximity with others, but not in heart connection. The Lord, on the other hand, does not want people in the same room as each other, as much as he wants a deep sharing of heart, mind and purpose (Philippians 2:2). This can only happen when humility is present and when the example of the Lord Jesus is understood and followed (Philippians 2:3-11).

One outworking of the spiritual wave of repentance and prayer sweeping over us in the early 2000s was to challenge pride, fear, prejudice and ambition. In its place would grow mutual respect, acceptance of each other, support for one another and unity in the Holy Spirit. This did not mean that differences ceased to exist. Leaders and people still belonged to diverse denominational congregations. Variations of doctrine continued and flavours of worship-style persisted. Difference in personality and experience remained as surely as diversity of nationality, skin-colour and gender. What was different, however, was that such differences ceased to matter as much as they had done previously, if at all.

From this heart of love for God and appreciation of each other, grew stronger relationships that could bring strength, release the amazing power of synergy, provide support in good times and bad, and foster an atmosphere of mutual accountability. Such friendships outlast changes in circumstance and leadership role, and prove hugely helpful in the long term.

It would be absurd to claim that all Christians and church leaders in North Staffordshire were involved in the 2C7 journey. On the contrary, many Christians across the conurbation chose, for a whole variety of reasons, not to engage with the prayer movement. We have to be careful not to imagine that the Lord's work can be contained in just one 'box' or place. Even when a spiritual renewal is taking place, some will not be able to connect to it. This does not detract from the reality of the blessing received by those who joined the 2C7 movement. Nor does it necessarily indicate that those who chose not to engage with 2C7 were being disobedient to the Lord.

Limiting perspectives

The fourth of the seven values we adopted was, **'The kingdom of God impacts every aspect of personal and corporate life.'** From the earliest days of the 2C7 movement, the Lord underlined to us the breadth, size and scope of his work in the city. In view of this, there is no room for narrow-mindedness among God's people, because the Lord's purpose and power cannot be limited in any way. The dimensions of his thinking far exceed our own in their height, width and depth (Isaiah 55:8-9).

In some, however, a real sense of narrowness was in evidence. One reason for this is the historic certainty of Christian denominations concerning the correctness of their own doctrines and forms of worship. The inference that a particular set of beliefs or a particular style of meeting was the right – maybe the only – way to do things has often been implicit, if not explicit. There is amazing strength in corporate traditions. It can be tempting to believe that God works only through people and churches like our own.

Another limiting perspective is that God is at work only in and among Christian people. Such a belief severely limits vision concerning the range, scope and location of God's work. If we don't expect the Lord to be working in the arenas of daily life, we will not look for the evidence of his activity in such places. The clear testimony of the New Testament is that God's heart and purpose are not confined to church or to Christian meetings. The Lord is at work in individuals and communities, in homes and streets, as well as in church gatherings.

A further form of narrowness is the strength of parochialism inherent in Potteries' culture. Any town or city can be sub-divided into smaller communities and neighbourhoods, of course. In Stoke-on-Trent, however, the smallness of the geographic size of the identifiable areas, coupled with the strength of people's commitment to those localities, seems to belong to a different order to parochialism in other places. Therefore, people in Stoke-on-Trent can be tempted to believe that life revolves around their small corner of the city.

Kingdom vision

If these various cultural mind-sets remain unchallenged and unchanged, spiritual vision is severely impaired and faith for answered prayer inhibited. In response to these potential inhibiting factors, therefore, we attempted to maintain a wide prayer focus on the whole of life in the whole of the city. This meant seeking God for blessing on teachers and students at every level of education – nursery, primary, secondary and tertiary. It meant praying for National Health Service staff and for patients in hospitals and surgeries. It meant asking God to help managers and workers in offices and factories around the city.

Over the years we prayed for city councillors, for City Council managers and staff members. We prayed for the police service, for commerce and for business, for young people and for old people, for private enterprise, for judges and for lawyers, for prisoners and for ex-offenders, for footballers and for pop stars. In prayer we spanned neighbourhoods as well as the whole conurbation; suburbs and the city centre. We focused on local and regional issues; on national and international concerns as contemporary needs presented themselves.

No subject was off limits. The focus of prayer was deliberately and repeatedly on community and city matters.

Heal the Land

The prayer was always enveloped within a context of worship. The requests were mixed with faith. The aim was nothing short of the healing of the land of the City of Stoke-on-Trent and the surrounding conurbation. Humanly speaking, grounds for optimism were not always high, but the eye of faith reached out for the revelation of the glory of God in the transformation of the city.

6: EMPOWERMENT, COMMITMENT AND FLEXIBILITY

In the previous chapter I focused on the first four of the seven 2C7 values adopted to describe what the Lord was doing among us. Intimacy with God, Christian character, strong relationships and wide vision were evident and essential features of our corporate journey. The remaining three values address the issues of leadership, of long-term commitment and of the necessity of flexibility in view of God's sovereignty. These values form the content of this chapter.

Minister or leader?
The fifth 2C7 value was, **'Leaders who empower all God's people are the key to the future.'** This value statement recognised the vital role that Christian leaders play within Christian congregations and groups, as leaders do in any established group or organisation, of whatever type or focus. Within a Christian context, leaders are called to be the Christ-like, facilitative releasers of all God's people. They are the conductors of the orchestra, uniting God's people together into a functioning team, bringing out the best in each individual and creating a symphony of worship and witness to the greatness of God.

Sadly the reality on the ground may not always match up to the Biblical revelation. While the title and detailed function of ministers varies within and between denominations, Roman Catholic priests, Church of England vicars, Methodist ministers and Free-Church pastors are expected to play out what is essentially the same leadership role in their congregations. In this well-defined, culturally-embedded position, ministers are expected to simultaneously fulfil many different roles. They are to be the leaders in terms of setting the tone and direction of the congregation, the managers in terms of working with staff members and volunteers, the administrators who organise structure and detail, the chairs of teams and committees, the chief fundraisers of ongoing finance and special appeals, and the representatives of the church at public events. They are also the doers of many of the church's ministries, being the chief preachers, teachers, presidents and pastoral visitors.

For so much to be focused in and through one person is unhealthy, of course, in that no one person could ever possess all the gifts required to fulfil these multiple tasks, let alone have the mental ability to focus on them all, or the time to do them all well. It is also very unhelpful because it does not allow the multiplicity of gifts present within every congregation or group to develop and find their expression. I also believe that it is unholy, in that it works against the will of God, who has revealed his purpose to build his church through effective leadership, not to build his church to create roles for church leaders.

Vision and influence

This is not to say that leadership is not important. By definition leaders are vital to the future. But it is the proper understanding and outworking of the empowering nature of gifted leadership that will make the difference, rather than the continuation of a culturally-clichéd leadership role. For, in essence, the gift of leadership is simple. A leader is someone who has the ability to envisage a God-given future and to influence people towards the attainment of that vision.

The specific gift of leadership is the ability to see what others cannot and do not see. Vision is the power to perceive the big picture, the wider context and, above all, the future dimension of purpose. Embracing a different future leads to the development of programmes and projects that will ensure arrival at the destination, not those that perpetuate inherited traditions. Unless there is within the church the ability and the urgency to imagine the future, the congregation(s) will be condemned to wander around in circles and its members destined to experience only frustration and disillusionment.

Coupled with the leaders' ability to see comes the ability to build long-term relationships in order to influence people towards the fulfilment of the vision that is perceived. A vision without any connection to the present is destined forever to remain just a dream, however wonderful that dream may be. Moving a group of committed volunteers towards a mutually beneficial goal is a demanding task in itself, not to be undertaken by the faint-hearted!

Gifted Christian leaders are facilitative, not controlling. They do not, indeed cannot, order people to do anything. Nor can they exercise undue, coercive pressure on people. Leaders are not bullies. Rather they have to pave the way for others by the clarity of their vision, the example of their faith, the discipline of their behaviour, the logic of their argument and the power of their love for God's people.

Empowering service

Christian leaders treat their followers with great respect, believing in them, loving them, partnering with them, serving them, praising them and releasing them to be what the Lord has called them to be. This requires the investment of time and energy on the part of the leader, as well as of the disciple. Leadership is giving not taking, delegating not requiring, empowering not demanding, in short, flowing outwards to the people rather than inwards towards the leaders. Such empowering leaders are desperately needed today, because the result of their forward-looking, outward-focused, permission-giving, self-effacing service will be the growth, empowerment and release of God's people to be what they are called to be and to do what they are called to do.

Specifically, Christians enjoying the benefits of good leadership will be encouraged and trusted to develop their own intimacy with God the Father through Jesus Christ, to grow in Christ-like character and to build strong and lasting relationships with God's people. They will look for the kingdom of God in daily life and witness for the Lord in their own spheres of influence. They will understand what their own God-given gifts are and will be confident to use them in an appropriate way. As this takes place, Stoke-on-Trent will be amazed at the emergence of a humble, loving, intentional, confident, bold and sacrificial body of people – the church of Jesus Christ that nothing can overpower (Matthew 16:18).

Constant change

The penultimate 2C7 value was, **'Arrival at the destination demands commitment in the long term.'** This statement recognised the fact that quick-fixes and easy solutions are rarely to be found – and surely never in the context of a city of 230,000 people. As in any such area, life in Stoke-on-Trent operates through an amazingly complex series of interactions – geographic, cultural, social, educational, political and spiritual. The multi-dimensional nature of modern society tends to fragment, compartmentalise and diffuse daily life and to militate against shared values, mindsets and lifestyles.

Historically the potters of Tunstall and Burslem, Fenton and Longton experienced life in similar ways and viewed things through common lenses. Now, however, diversity of ethnicity, language, religion, education, experience and expectation is so great that nothing can be taken-as-read across the population in the conurbation. Added to all this is the fact that, in the 21st Century, nothing is expected to last long and that everything is constantly changing, whether cars or clothes, gadgets or machines, jobs or relationships. At such a time, the concept of committing to a vision and goals for the long term seems decidedly antiquated.

Firm commitment
Yet the call of Jesus is to take stock and then to make an informed commitment to the ongoing pursuit of the kingdom of God (Luke 14:28-33). Once such a commitment has been made and the journey commenced, a follower of Jesus is challenged to stick to it at all costs, without wavering. To look back is to render oneself unfit for the kingdom of God (Luke 9:62).

This unshakeable commitment to God is mirrored most powerfully in life-long commitment to a person's spouse. Marriage as we have understood and experienced it in our society is a Christian institution. Consequently it is no surprise that, as our nation has turned its back on its historic commitment to Christ and to Christian faith, it has also turned its back on Christian marriage. Inexorably divorce rates continue to rise and co-habitation increases, inevitably resulting in the breakdown of relationships and of family life itself. The emotional and psychological damage done to our children, and our children's children, is almost too painful to imagine. The huge and tragic cost to our society, both now and in the future, cannot be calculated.

Firm commitment to God is also echoed in ongoing determination to seek the kingdom of God on earth in the transformation of town, city and nation. For this we pray each time we say the familiar words taught by the Lord Jesus, 'your kingdom come, your will be done on earth as it is in heaven' (Matthew 6:10).

Embarking on a journey of vision and faith is full of potential and possibility. The start of the race is filled with anticipation and inspiration. It is invigorating and exhilarating. It will not always remain so! Surprises and shocks await. Highs and lows abound. Breakthroughs and blessings are as sure as setbacks and disappointments. Sometimes the journey is light and hopes are high. More often life is simply the daily grind of prayer and faith, with nothing dramatically good or bad. At other points we seem to hit a brick wall of opposition and challenge, with no possibility of forward progress. Even more strength-sapping than outright opposition can be the tiredness brought on by unrealised expectations, for 'hope deferred makes the heart sick...' (Proverbs 13:12).

So once in a while we may even ponder whether the journey is worthwhile. Privately we may wonder why those not committed to seeking God's kingdom seem to have such an easier and better life than we do. Facing this challenge and asking such questions is not new. The 3,000-years-old poems and songs of the Old Testament Psalms reflect exactly the same internal struggles. For example, Psalm 73 was written by Asaph during a time of total despair and therefore speaks openly about his inability to keep a correct perspective on the big picture, until re-focusing on the glory of the Lord.

Eternal perspective
Knowing how to respond to times of tiredness and despair is, therefore, all-important. The strength to carry on comes through rock-solid commitment to the God who promises always to be with us (Matthew 28:20) and never to abandon us, whatever the circumstances (Hebrews 13:5). Jesus himself

promised to send the Holy Spirit from God the Father to be our guide and supporter, teacher and friend (John 14:16-18).

Heaven-sent comfort and strength is often transmitted to us through human relationships. Thus it is really important to have as many Christian friends as possible and, among them, a small core of deeper, closer, long-term confidants. True friends bring hope and encouragement, support and comfort. They are not afraid to challenge when we are stepping out of line and into danger. They do not shy away from bringing correction and encouraging restoration when necessary. It is impossible to maintain long-term commitment without them.

Armed with unassailable commitment and supported by fellow-travellers, the journey continues. By God's grace, vision will be realised and goals attained. In some cases, however, the full realisation of the vision may be reserved for future generations. God's work is not limited to us and to our life-span. Prayers we pray and work we do may be seed which will not bear fruit until after our own passing into eternity.

This calls for a greater degree of trust in God, as we come to realise that others may reap what we sow, but decide to carry on anyway, knowing that sowing and reaping are all the work of God (1 Corinthians 3:6-9). We follow our 'father' Abraham, who lived and died in faith, without ever seeing the realisation of the promises God gave him (Hebrews 11:8-10). Abraham came to the place of trust and commitment to the long-term, not just in relationship to one or two future generations, but to the eternal purpose of God.

Let God be God

The seventh and final 2C7 value was, **'God often works beyond the parameters of our understanding and experience.'** This value statement recognised and celebrated the fact that the God of heaven and earth cannot

81

be confined in the small box of our experience and expectation. He is the sovereign Lord over all. It is too easy for us to attempt to tie God down to a programme or a process. Whatever our motives for doing so, the very idea that we could, or should, seek to define God is fraught with danger. For, if we could completely define God's nature, encapsulate his purpose and formularise his activity, we would by definition be as great as God.

Yet the sovereign Lord is by nature transcendent, that is, far above and beyond our dimension of being, thinking and doing (Isaiah 55:8-9). There are no limits to his intellect and no boundaries to his power (Isaiah 40:25-28). He does not need external help or require support in order to exist and to do. He is who and what he is. He is the great 'I am' who does not change from one generation to another, but who remains eternally and essentially the same (Exodus 3:14).

Therefore, any attempt to define or confine the Lord is self-evidently doomed to failure. We simply cannot tell God what he can or cannot do, how he will do what he does, or whom he can or cannot use. All of us have inherited or received an understanding of Christian faith and experience through a specific lens. Leaders belonging to our mother congregation or denomination may well have taught us much that it is good, but no one person or denomination can claim to have sole access to the fulness of divine truth. We simply cannot afford to judge people who belong to different church families than our own, or to exclude them from the over-arching embrace of God's love. We should not be tempted to imagine that we are the special recipients of divine favour. The Lord loves the whole church, not just parts of it, and gives himself to it as a bridegroom to his bride (Ephesians 5:25-27).

Furthermore, we cannot decide that our own understanding about a particular doctrine is complete and correct to the exclusion of all other interpretations. We can be sure about fundamental Christian beliefs, such as the fact that Christ will return to earth once again, but we cannot be dogmatic about the exact details and precise timings related to his return. We have to leave room for our own paucity of understanding and for the transcendent sovereignty of God.

Nor can we afford to imagine that the Lord confines himself to working only and always within the confines of the body of Christ. Yes, the Lord loves the church and longs to work through it, but to think that he cannot work beyond its boundaries is theologically and experientially incorrect. In the words of a well-known Bible verse, 'God so loved the world that he gave his one and only Son...' (John 3:16). None of this means that there is no place for Bible study and scripture teaching, for certainties and principles, for guidelines and disciplines. On the contrary, some things can be very clearly understood. What it does mean is that we cannot be prescriptive and dogmatic about everything. We must leave room for God's immensity and time for his eternity!

Embracing mystery

So, on the 2C7 journey, we chose to embrace the fact that the Lord works in ways that are hidden from our understanding, not because he is hiding in the darkness of immorality or corruption, but because the wisdom of his ways is hidden from our limited comprehension. We determined to celebrate the mystery of the divine unknown and unknowable. We decided to accept that some of God's ways seem fuzzy and undefined to us. We acknowledged the reality that we were sometimes surprised, occasionally shocked, regularly amazed and often awestruck at the sovereign purpose of God outworked in the world.

We further determined to keep our hearts and minds as open as possible to other people, to different perspectives, to diversity of worship styles and to new ways of being. We aimed to remain flexible in our thinking and adaptable in our methodology. By doing so, we occasionally made mistakes, but often discovered open doors to the future and to undiscovered paths to the unknown greatness of God.

We believed, and still believe, that the Lord is working to refine, renew and prepare his people for the next chapter in his unfolding story of regeneration and renewal. This next stage of the journey will inevitably involve a fresh revelation of God's glory and demand a fresh response of faith and obedience from his people. The truth that 'God often works beyond the parameters of our understanding and experience' was worthy of inclusion in our values statement, and remains so to this day. God is God, and we seek to celebrate the overwhelming mystery of his majesty.

These seven foundational values became a useful foundation and guide to us on our journey or humility and prayer. They proved to be clear and concise, relevant and helpful. They accurately described the work that the Lord was doing among us, without confining us to a particular doctrine or worship style, or committing us to particular programmes and agendas.

7: FUEL AND FOCUS

In its early days, the 2C7 prayer movement was carried along on a tidal wave of fervour and excitement. A tidal wave does not continue in the long term, however, but begins to subside once it reaches an obstacle or starts to move inland. The only way that the wave can maintain its momentum is to find a focused channel along which to course and/or a new source of energy to power it onwards.

This same transition process had to take place within the 2C7 prayer movement. The early months of excitement had to make way for the focus, momentum and maturity of an ongoing prayer agenda. The change from passion to focused purpose had to be handled with wisdom and care, and the newly-focused movement had to be supported and promoted with vision and energy. This chapter deals with the fuel for prayer and the focus of prayer.

Intercessory prayer

The church of Jesus Christ is called to be a body of intercessors, the people who stand between heaven and earth, linking God and humankind. Christians are people who hear from heaven and speak to earth, and who lift earth to heaven in prayer and praise. In this matter, they follow the lead of their Lord Jesus Christ, who was the perfect mediator between God and human beings (1 Timothy 2:1-6).

In practice, some believers are more aware of a specific call to intercessory prayer, and apparently more gifted for its specific task, than other Christians are. We call those people who give themselves more fully to a life of listening and speaking, waiting and groaning in prayer, by the descriptive name 'intercessors.' Intercessors are the unsung heroes of the church, the unnamed and generally unknown people who faithfully and without public acclaim lay down their lives day by day to conduct the business of heaven on earth. Such intercessory prayers may be unknown on earth, but they are well-known in heaven.

In the early days of the 2C7 journey, local Methodist Pat Miles acted as our intercessory prayer co-ordinator. In time, her leading role was taken by Pentecostal Rosa Warrilow, whose long period of sickness and subsequent death on 29 February 2008 left a large hole in the 2C7 prayer team. Lloyd and I greatly appreciated and respected the group of intercessory women (supplemented by the occasional man!). We invited them to attend the monthly Monday morning Christian leaders' prayer meetings. They would participate in the opening worship and prayer alongside the leaders, before quietly slipping away in order to pray in private in another part of the Bethel Christian Centre building.

The intercessors would then pray for the church leaders, for the meeting taking place and for the city generally. From these intercessory prayer times, reports and prophetic pictures were regularly submitted back to Lloyd and me for our consideration. Often the reports and messages proved to be timely, relevant and confirmatory. Eternity alone will reveal the full story of the impact of the band of faithful intercessors.

Prolonged intercession

Intercession is not just about the length of time spent in prayer, although those who do commit to longer periods of prayer are more likely to discover more consistently the heart of God. So it was that in early 2003 Rosa Warrilow and Sara Jukes, both based at Bethel Christian Centre, began to hold a whole night of prayer on the second Friday of each month. The overnight prayer vigils began at 10.00pm on the Friday evening and concluded at 7.00am on the Saturday morning. They were given the name 'Night Watch.' Each month the Night Watch meetings were publicised at 2C7 prayer meetings. The Night Watch events ran until mid-2005 and played a very supportive role to the 2C7 vision. They were never large in attendance, but were deep in quality, wide in vision and clear in focus.

Alongside the Night Watch meetings, whole weeks of unbroken prayer were introduced. The first week of prayer was launched out of the monthly 2C7 prayer meeting on Wednesday 29 January 2003 and ran without pause until midnight at the end of the following Wednesday, 5 February. Sara Jukes co-ordinated the event by inviting local churches to take responsibility for a six-hour slot during the seven days of unbroken prayer. These church slots were supplemented by the involvement of intercessory groups and individuals.

A prayer chapel was set aside at the Bethel Christian Centre building for the use of those taking part in the prayer push. Over the week, the room was filled up with specific written prayer requests, notes containing answers to prayer, scripture verses and drawings produced by those who find art to be a wonderful expression of the act of intercession. A second week of prayer was held in late 2003 and a third in July 2004.

Unbroken prayer
The three separate weeks of unbroken prayer held in 2003 and 2004 led to the desire to organise a month of unbroken prayer by Christians from across the conurbation, focusing on the healing of the land. During the autumn of 2004, the Saltbox took the lead in preparing the first month of prayer, which was scheduled to take place in January 2005.

The month of prayer was constructed in the following way. Local churches and Christian organisations were approached and each asked to commit to one 24-hour period of unbroken prayer during the month. The churches were given freedom to meet for their prayer day in their local church building, in a church hall or other suitable venue. The recommendation was that nobody should be left to carry the prayer burden alone, unless unavoidable. Attention was to be given to security for the overnight prayer slots, especially if a public building was being used for this purpose.

The starting and ending point for each prayer 'day' was set at 8.00pm, a time which allowed each church to begin and end their commitment with a corporate hour of prayer much more easily than if the 24 hours began and ended at midnight. Congregations and organisations were allowed complete freedom to worship and pray according to their own tradition and style. In this way, charismatic churches could take responsibility for a day of prayer as much as High Church Anglican parishes, and Evangelical congregations could participate alongside Pentecostal churches.

United intercession

What mattered to us was not the style of prayer, but the focus of the intercession. In this we were helped by Dan Epley, a Christian leader from Asheville, North Carolina, who became a friend of the 2C7 journey through his regular visits to Longton Elim Church. Dan inspired us to write down three prayer themes for the month, which were summarised by the titles harvest, healing and worship.

Under the heading of harvest, we were praying for increasing numbers of people to come to faith in Jesus Christ. The title healing helped us to pray for God's healing power on individual people, congregations and on the land. The heading worship represented the prayer request for a deeper experience of the presence and glory of God to be revealed among God's people.

Well over 30 church congregations and groups signed up for the first month of unbroken prayer in January 2005. Of the churches taking part, 16 were Anglican, eleven Pentecostal or charismatic, three Methodist and one Salvation Army. As well as the participating congregations, United Christian Broadcasters took responsibility for one day, as did North Staffs Youth for Christ, Keele University Christian Union and Churches Together in Biddulph.

In most cases, one church or group took responsibility for a whole 24-hour period, though two of the larger churches took two days each and four of the smaller churches took half a day each. Communication and interest was maintained through the month by Cross Rhythms City Radio, which provided an update about the prayer month on air at 12.30pm and 4.30pm each day.

Months of prayer
From the very beginning, local church leaders began to share the stories of God's blessing on their congregations through engaging in the month of prayer. One Pentecostal Church leader reported that 58 different church members had taken part in its 24-hour period of prayer, some staying for one hour, others for 12 hours. Participants had been invited to sign a prayer book and had written many positive comments. Another congregation reported that 'The 24-hour prayer day was AWESOME x7.' Many of the churches had created different prayer stations around their room(s), releasing much creativity in terms of drawing, pottery, materials and visual aids to prayer. The overall and overwhelming response to the month of prayer was that everyone had appreciated the event and everyone wanted to do it again.

Accordingly, work began almost immediately to plan a second month of prayer to take place in June 2005. The format and focus of the prayer month echoed that of the January month of prayer, though on this occasion the area encompassed by the participants was not limited to the North Staffordshire conurbation alone. Other towns within the Trent Valley area of Staffordshire were now included, with a day of prayer being taken by Churches Together in Stone, another day by churches in Uttoxeter and three days being provided by churches in Burton-upon-Trent.

A third month of united, unbroken prayer took place in February 2006, in the run-up to the second united healing mission.[1] A fourth month of prayer covered the 31 days of May 2007, when 36 churches and organisations covered the month in unbroken prayer. This particular month was chosen to coincide with the Trumpet Call national prayer event at the NEC arena in Birmingham on Saturday 19 May and the international Global Day of Prayer on Sunday 27 May.

In addition to these two much wider larger prayer events, two dates at the end of May 2007 pointed us to the unlimited power of the Holy Spirit. Sunday 27 May was the annual reminder of the first outpouring of the Holy Spirit on the Day of Pentecost, which had resulted in the birth of the worldwide church of Jesus Christ. Thursday 31 May 2007 carried a strong local resonance in that it was the 200th anniversary of the outpouring of the Holy Spirit at Mow Cop, just to the north of the city, which launched the deeply-impacting and widely-reverberating revival movement known as Primitive Methodism.

Prayer and fasting
A final period of unbroken prayer during the 2C7 era took

---

[1] The healing missions of 2005/2006 are described in Chapter 9.

place in April and May 2008. This time of prayer was different to what had preceded it in two significant ways. Firstly, the length of the season of prayer was extended from 30 to 40 days. These 40 days began on Tuesday 1 April and concluded on Saturday 10 May, the day before the Day of Pentecost in that year. The second difference was that people were encouraged to add fasting to their prayers.

Prayer and fasting has a strong Biblical pedigree, having been exercised by people such as Anna the intercessor (Luke 2:37), John the Baptist and his disciples (Mark 2:18), and the Lord Jesus himself (Matthew 4:2). The leaders of the church in Antioch fasted and prayed before sending out Barnabas and Saul on their missionary journey (Acts 13:2-3). They in turn fasted before appointing elders in the churches they planted (Acts 14:23).

Adding fasting to prayer has the effect of removing distractions and facilitating a stronger focus on the Lord. It demonstrates commitment and urgency on the part of the person doing the fasting, and hones the spiritual senses to feel the heartbeat of God. Biblical teaching and Christian experience unite in their testimony to the breakthrough power of God at work in response to seasons of prayer and fasting.

Time to embrace

Some time in early 2007, the Lord put it into the heart of 2C7 worship leader Paul Critchley that we should spend some time together simply worshipping the Lord over the city. The germ of the idea that would become 'Embrace' was born. In its developed form, a 12-hour period of unbroken worship would take place at the Bethel Christian Centre from 9.30am to 9.30pm on Saturday 20 October 2007.

Eight different bands and worship leaders from local churches were invited to lead worship for 90 minutes each. Paul Critchley led the first half hour plus the last hour of

worship, pray, sit, reflect
Saturday 20 October 2007
9.30am - 9.30pm

2007

embrace

12HR UNBROKEN WORSHIP

Drinks available throughout the day
Venue: Bethel Christian Centre, Leek Road, Abbey Hulton, S-o-T. ST2 8BY
More info: Saltbox Christian Centre
Email: email@saltbox.org.uk
Web: www.saltbox.org.uk
Tel: 01782 207200

the twelve. There was much diversity within the groups and worship leaders. Some had a band of several members. One worship leader played an acoustic guitar alone. One band had dancers and banners. Alongside the worship led from the platform, space was created to sit and reflect, or to engage in creative arts. The event was interspersed with a few spoken prayers and Bible readings, but there was no preaching. The focus of the Embrace event was 'from us to God,' not 'from God to us.'

Outward focus

Thus the prayer seasons undertaken under the umbrella of 2C7 varied in length from an hour or two to 40 days. The prayer styles went from High Church to Pentecostal and the prayer contexts embraced the personal and private, as well as the many hundreds in a large gathering. Prayer took place in homes and along river banks, through city streets and in church buildings.

The focus of the prayer, however, can be summarised within the last phrase of 2 Chronicles 7:14, that the Lord would 'heal the land.' That is, the end purpose of the repentance, humility and prayer of the people of God was not for their own personal blessing, but that the land would be healed. For us, this meant carrying a vision for the glory of God to be revealed in the healing of the City of Stoke-on-Trent, along with the neighbouring Borough of Newcastle-under-Lyme and the surrounding areas of the Staffordshire Moorlands. Our prayer was not for the revival of the local churches, but for the revitalisation of the stalling local economy, the improvement of educational achievement across the board and a dramatic increase in the health of local residents. We were seeking the Lord for an invigoration in local party politics and a new energy in local arts and media.

Since this was the aim, we made regular invitations to local leaders from the world of business, education, healthcare and politics to attend our meetings and to address us with first-hand information about the area as a means of fuelling our prayers. Over the years we were visited by the head teachers of local schools, police inspectors and superintendents, prison managers, the director of the Local Strategic Partnership, the Chief Executive of the City Council, local political party leaders, MPs and the Elected Mayor of Stoke-on-Trent.

Answered prayer
Inevitably we asked those leaders addressing our meetings for their top 'prayer requests' for the area, which must have posed an interesting challenge for those leaders who did not profess any Christian faith. None of those present will forget the evening when a political leader, returning to speak to us for the third time, thanked us for our prayers, because

as an atheist he acknowledged that prayers were indeed being answered!

Another visitor to a 2C7 prayer meeting was Mike Sassi, editor of the large-circulation local newspaper, the Sentinel. During his visit at the prayer meeting held on Wednesday 27 June 2007, Mike's three prayer requests were the emergence of high profile visionary leadership in the city, a change away from negative thinking and premiership football. We promised Mike, as we did all our visitors, that we would pray over these issues. The prayer request about premiership football in North Staffs was easy to understand, since it would raise the profile of the city nationally and internationally, as well as improve morale within the city.

The problem was that there are two local football clubs, Stoke City FC and Port Vale FC, and we were not sure if a prayer for one was a prayer against the other! Nonetheless, we were all more than thrilled when, at the end of the season that began in August 2007, just six weeks after Sassi's visit to the prayer meeting, Stoke City was promoted from the Championship to the Premier League on the afternoon of Sunday 4 May 2008, following a 0-0 draw against Leicester City. Nobody, locally or nationally, had predicted a Stoke City promotion prior to the start of the season, making the event even more noteworthy from our perspective.

This was not the first and only occasion when specific prayer targets produced remarkable results. On Wednesday 31 March 2004 we were visited by Sue Sinclair, who leads a prayer initiative in Liverpool called Drugsnet. Through Drugsnet, Sue and her network of friends pray regularly about the issue of drug abuse in and around Merseyside. They also keep in touch with the police to offer support and encouragement to them. During her visit, Sue mentioned publicly the major issue of drugs arriving in

Liverpool destined for the North Staffordshire area. In response to Sue's comments, we prayed together at the meeting about the situation. Just one week later, on Thursday 8 April 2004, £35million worth of cannabis resin was discovered in containers at the docks in Liverpool. As a result, seven people were arrested, one from Walsall, one from Liverpool and five from Stoke-on-Trent.[2]

Who says that God does not hear and answer prayer! The key seems to be to rediscover a focus on the land, the place of your calling, and then to commit to pray with as many others of God's people as possible for the healing of the land. Once the commitment has been made, the next key is not to let go and not to give up, but rather to keep fuelling the fire until the prayers are answered and the land is healed.

---

[2] This made front page headlines in *The Sentinel* newspaper on Thursday 15 April 2004.

8: BUILDING NETWORKS

The energy and focus of a prayer movement, as indeed of any people movement, is sustained and built by the dynamic of its relationships. For a prayer movement, relations begin and centre on the relationship with the living God as of primary importance. From this hub emanates the relationships that flow among and between Christian leaders and people. Strong relationships produce life, balance, freshness, momentum and focus. To remove oneself from the orbit of fresh and growing relationships leads inevitably to isolation, aberration and stagnation.

In essence, Christian faith is a corporate entity. Good and committed relationships are a necessity, not an add-on extra. Existing relationships have to be maintained and deepened over time, if they are to remain fresh and productive. This requires the expenditure of time and effort! Alongside the development of existing friendships, new connections have to be made constantly, with the hope and intention that each one will lead to a significant friendship, whether in the short-, medium-, or long-term.

The 2C7 journey was greatly helped by the strength of relational connections within North Staffordshire, as well as those which extended regionally, nationally and internationally. Life flowed into and out from the monthly meetings to touch many people, both locally and beyond.

2C7 'on the road'

Two years into the 2C7 journey, the idea was proposed to take 2C7-style meetings on the road to local churches. This was first attempted on Sunday evening 21 September 2003 at the Parish Church of St Mary the Virgin, Bucknall, mother church of a large parish, which counted three other churches within the parish boundaries, alongside itself.[1] The prayer meeting was conducted in the style of 2C7 meetings by Lloyd Cooke, Paul Critchley and me, albeit with a focus on prayer for the Bucknall Parish area and people.

Following the success of this venture, other similar meetings were soon held at St Mary's, Trentham, at Port Vale Football Club and at Birches Head Christian Fellowship. Three more local church meetings were held in 2004, at Longton Elim Church, at St John the Baptist Anglican Church, Wetley Rocks, and at Wesley Hall Methodist Church, Sneyd Green. A final 2C7 'on the road' was held at St Luke's Parish Church, Endon, in March 2005.

Traditional setting

Although the 2C7 meetings adopted a gentle charismatic flavour and style, not every pastor or congregation member attending the prayer meetings came personally from that background. One or two Church of England vicars involved in the prayer journey suggested holding a special 2C7 prayer meeting in a style that would enable those with a more traditional church approach to engage with the 2C7 prayer movement.

The Right Reverend Christopher Hill (Bishop of Stafford), the Venerable Godfrey Stone (Archdeacon of Stoke-upon

---

[1] Since that time, one of the four churches belonging to Bucknall Parish, St Chad's Bagnall, has become part of the Endon St Luke's Parish.

Trent), Rev. John Walker (Chester and Stoke-on-Trent Methodist District Superintendent) and Father Pat McKinney (Roman Catholic Auxiliary Bishop of Birmingham) were all keen to run with the concept and aided the planning of the service. Therefore, on Friday 27 February 2004, during the season of Lent, a joint service of humility and repentance was led by the senior churchmen of the area. More than 70 church leaders attended the event, many of whom did not feel comfortable with the style of the ongoing monthly 2C7 prayer events.

The style of service was indeed very different to that normally on offer, including, for example, a lengthy written order of service. However, the same spirit of humility and reconciliation was present. The service was sincere and significant. Apart from the spiritual impact, relationships were strengthened across the practical barriers that exist between people who worship in widely diverse types of styles.

Retreat to advance
After almost a year of the 2C7 journey, we decided to hold a day's retreat for the dozen church leaders most strongly committed to the vision. This short retreat would provide opportunity to reflect on what the Lord had done and to consider direction for the future. The retreat was held in September 2002 at Rudyard Methodist Church, a few miles outside the city.

The desire for the core group of 2C7 leaders to spend more time together in prayer and fellowship led to a 24-hour retreat held over two days in June 2003 at Shallowford House, the Lichfield Diocesan Conference Centre. These longer times of prayer, reflection, intercession, fellowship, food and fun were to become an integral and highly important part of the ongoing 2C7 journey.

Eleven further retreats were held at Shallowford House between October 2003 and November 2008. On average, 20 church leaders were in attendance at each retreat. The criterion for invitation was simply the degree of connectedness to the 2C7 vision and journey at that time. This meant, of course, that there was a degree of change in the personnel involved in the retreats over the years, as some leaders connected into 2C7, or conversely ceased to be involved.

Perhaps more than any other of the many meetings held under the auspices of the 2C7 movement, the Shallowford-based retreats provided the opportunity to go deeper with God together and afforded the time to hear from the Lord as a group. The events served also as a wonderful occasion for relationship-building and social interaction, alongside the more directly spiritual activities.

Old Staffordshire

At various times and for various reasons, during the 1990s Lloyd and I had come to know some of the Christian leaders based in Birmingham, men such as Bob Dunnett, Bryan Pullinger, Nick Cuthbert and Ian Cole, who carried a vision for Birmingham (and beyond), as well as for their own specific church or ministry. In the early 2000s, Lloyd had also come into contact with some leaders who were leading united prayer in and for the Black Country.

Early in 2004, we arranged a meeting of some of the prayer leaders from North Staffordshire, the Black Country and Birmingham. The first gathering took place on Tuesday 6 July 2004 in Walsall. A further meeting was convened in February 2005. On both occasions it was significant to meet together as people from the historic county of Staffordshire, which had until a century ago included Wolverhampton, West Bromwich, Walsall and the northern suburbs of Birmingham within its borders.

Although these official meetings did not continue in this format, the relationships built by them did, being developed and strengthened by further conversations, contacts and meetings under a variety of different headings. It has been fascinating to see the different ways in which the journey of vision, humility and prayer has developed in each place, while stemming in each case from the same heart to see the land healed.

Connecting the Connectors

One venue in which the leaders from Birmingham, the Black Country and Stoke-on-Trent have worked together has been the staging of 'Connecting the Connectors' conferences. The aim of these was to create a venue for those involved in city-wide, town-wide or regional inter-church ministry to gather for three days of inspiration, encouragement, teaching and reflection. The conferences of February 2007 and October 2008 were both held at Swanwick Conference Centre in Derbyshire.

Invitations were sent out around the country through the means of already-existing relational networks. No general advertising campaigns were run in the Christian press. What mattered most was that people invited people known to them to be present at the conference. In this, as in everything, relationships were the vital thing.

Another reason for adopting this approach was that the agenda was relatively new and undeveloped, and the gatherings were in the truest sense a conference – a place for sharing among friends. While some speakers were invited to address the conference, there was a clear understanding that some people have found some clues and have some stories to share, but that nobody yet saw the whole picture or had accomplished the job of entirely transforming their city or region. The two retreats were very successful in each bringing together around 50 people from all corners of England (plus a few from Scotland and Ireland!) to engage around the vision of the revelation of the glory of God and the healing of the land by the power of God.

Trumpet Call

Another way in which the connection between Stoke-on-Trent, Black Country and Birmingham leaders bore fruit was in the seven Trumpet Call prayer meetings that were staged at the National Exhibition Centre in Birmingham between 2005 and 2010. In line with the vision of Ian and Pauline Cole, leaders of the Birmingham-based World Prayer Centre, the Trumpet Call prayer events focused on the healing of the nation and drew together Christians from all corners of the British Isles in pursuit of this goal. An average of 4,000 people has attended each prayer day.

From the start, Lloyd became involved in planning and presenting the Trumpet Call prayer events. He played a strategic supportive role for Ian Cole in running the meetings and found doors of connection and networking open to him as a result of his involvement in the national prayer meetings. This led to many journeys around the country to share with Christians and with church leaders the story of what the Lord was doing in Stoke-on-Trent.

Invited guests

Through the seven years of the 2C7 journey, we invited relatively few national or international leaders to visit the area with a view to speaking at the corporate gatherings. We were very clear in our minds that we would not use our large gatherings simply as a reason to invite well-known Christian leaders to speak. In the 2C7 movement, it was not title, reputation or supposed importance that mattered. What counted much more to us was that visitors were able to flow with us in humility of spirit around the focus on healing the land.

With that in mind, we were pleased to welcome as our speakers Bob Dunnett, longstanding prayer-for-the nation leader (Bob visited us in February 2003); Dennis Wrigley, inspirational leader of the Maranatha Community (Visited in March 2003); and Gerald Coates, leader of the Pioneer movement (June 2003). Ian Cole, leader of the World Prayer Centre, visited us in September 2004; his colleague Jane Holloway followed in June 2005. Malcolm Duncan, then director of Oasis-based FaithWorks, addressed the church leaders in November 2005; irrepressible and unconventional worship leader Godfrey Birtill led open prayer meetings in February 2007 and again in February 2008.

Unplanned connections

On other occasions visiting Christian leaders were brought to the 2C7 meetings by a locally-based priest or pastor. Many visitors from near and far passed through the meetings in this way over the seven years of 2C7 meetings. To take just one example, international visitors to the leaders' prayer meeting of Monday 24 October 2005 were John and Holly Roddam, and Paul and Beth Stadler (all from Washington State, USA), Carmelo di Marco and Stefano Canniota (from Palermo, of whom more to follow) and Jim Nightingale (Australia).

In a few instances, there was an instant-but-real meeting of hearts and minds, leading to an ongoing relationship between the visitor and local pastors. One such visitor was Dan Epley, a Christian leader from North Carolina, USA. Dan already enjoyed a long-standing partnership with Longton Elim Church and its leaders Phil and Sue Parsons. Dan became especially strongly connected to 2C7 during the healing missions of Autumn 2005 and Spring 2006, at which he was a committed, mature and inspirational helper. Dan also spoke powerfully and prophetically into several local churches in the area, and to the 2C7 leaders gathered on retreat at Shallowford House.

Florence Kanyati visited from Zimbabwe in 2005. The strength of her vision and commitment were evident to everyone. Florence made a strong connection with Rev. Sue Goodwin, vicar of St John the Baptist, Wetley Rocks, which eventually led Sue and her friend Marlene Bartlett to visit Florence and to preach in a number of churches in Harare in September 2006. Sue Goodwin has since maintained this connection with Florence and, through her, with the troubled nation of Zimbabwe.

The evangelist

Another such visitor to the area was Carmelo di Marco, leader of the large and thriving Church of God congregation in Palermo, capital of Sicily. Carmelo was already in a long-term partnership with John and Joan Alessi, who had previously served as missionaries in Palermo, but who were now back at home in North Staffordshire.

As mentioned, John brought Carmelo and his assistant Stefano Canniota to the 2C7 prayer meetings of late October 2005. Invited to introduce himself, Carmelo made an instant impact and found a ready welcome among the leaders and people. Three months later, John Alessi and I spent a week visiting Carmelo and preaching in Palermo. Carmelo has returned to Staffordshire on several occasions and a connection between church leaders in Palermo and Stoke-on-Trent has been established.

One point of connection between Palermo and Stoke-on-Trent is that Palermo is reputedly the worst city in Italy in terms of quality of life, just as Stoke-on-Trent had been so labelled in England and Wales in 2001. This created a certain amount of empathy and understanding between church leaders in the respective cities, understanding, as they do, the challenges to be faced to change the fortunes of the two cities and to heal their respective lands.

The bishop

A further example of a visitor who arrived unexpectedly at a leaders' prayer meeting was Eddie Mulenga, from Lusaka, Zambia. Eddie was brought along to the leaders' prayer meeting by Harold Goodwin in April 2007. The connection between 'Bishop' Eddie and the local leaders was immediate. Eddie was invited to speak at the monthly prayer meeting two days following his initial introduction, then at the leaders' prayer retreat at Shallowford House a week later in early May 2007. In addition, he preached powerfully in several local churches during his visit to the area.

Eddie, we discovered, led a group of churches in Zambia called the Liberty Christian Centre. He also played a role in national prayer events in the country, acted as chaplain to presidents and appeared regularly on television to speak on behalf of the Christian community. Bishop Eddie returned to Stoke-on-Trent in October 2008, just as 2C7 was coming to a close. He was granted an extensive itinerary among local churches and spoke clearly, relevantly and prophetically into many individuals, small groups and congregations.

The prophet

Perhaps the greatest ongoing impact into our 2C7 journey from the outside came in the person of Martin Scott, who first visited the area in November 2003. Martin's first visit to Stoke-on-Trent made a significant impact on him, as well as on us. In his own words:

> I became aware of 2C7 around 2003, around seven years after I had begun to realise that the only way forward was where believers were willing to develop relationships

for the sake of territory, not simply on the grounds of a common identity. When I first met with church leaders from the Stoke area I was immediately impacted that here was a group of people who carried that passion. They were humble in heart, ready to hear from one another, and focused on seeing God come to every aspect of their communities.[2]

From the very first visit, Martin spoke very prophetically to individuals and to the whole group. His accuracy in prophetic detail, that is, in addressing very specific facts and situations in the life of a person not known to him, was often astounding. Martin's ministry to us was not limited to that one aspect, however, wonderful as his direct prophetic revelation was. Martin proved to be a good friend, a humble servant, a supportive encourager and a willing listener. He was happy to sit alongside us just as much as to speak to us. Martin visited us at no fewer than five of the extended retreats held at Shallowford House between January 2004 and November 2007. He also visited the monthly 2C7 prayer events on five occasions between November 2003 and May 2008.

My interaction with them has made a lasting impact on me. I have realised that the consistent prayer (in diverse forms), the ongoing encouragement of one another, the re-iteration of a 'kingdom' (and not simply a 'church') vision, with an openness to prophetic input has helped 2C7 model something that cannot simply be copied, but could certainly serve as a template to be adapted in many other situations.

In these last few years the focus that 2C7 has had on the shape of their region beyond the four walls of church has been very refreshing. As they have pursued

---

[2] E-mail from Martin Scott, 7 March 2011.

prayer, relationships and action into the sectors that shape their communities, they are helping position God's people for the transition that seems to be so necessary: the transition from simply exercising gifting inside the Christian community, to being willing servants of the wider community.[3]

Sadly, during much of Martin's journeying alongside us, his life was being touched by tragedy. His wife Sue contracted cancer and suffered ill-health for some time before her untimely death on 14 February 2005, at the early age of 52. Through all the suffering and subsequent bereavement, Martin never sought attention for himself, but was eager to serve. He is a remarkable man.

For each and every personal relationship and corporate network established and built during the 2C7 journey we are profoundly grateful. The Lord is in the work of establishing networks along which the energy of his Spirit can course. This was his work among us as we came together to seek his face in repentance, humility and prayer for the healing of the land. This leads us to the story of another divine connection which would have a far-reaching and dramatic impact on our 2C7 journey.

---

[3] E-mail from Martin Scott, 7 March 2011.

9: A TIME FOR HEALING

In the spring of 2005, Lloyd visited the south coast of England in order to fulfil a commitment made to a friend to preach in a couple of Methodist churches. During the trip, he was introduced to some other visitors who were there at the same time, New Zealanders Craig and Jenni Marsh.

Remarkable story

Craig and Jenni had been involved in various forms of Christian leadership for many years, but Craig had developed stomach cancer in the 1990s. He had undergone years of treatment in New Zealand, including several major operations and involving the removal of his stomach. This left Craig unable to eat properly and subject to frequent spasms and blackouts. Despite his weak condition, Craig had travelled whenever and wherever he could to be prayed for by Christian leaders with a proven healing ministry. However, the prayers for God's healing intervention went apparently unheeded and Craig's condition continued to deteriorate.

On 4 May 1999 Craig visited a conference of ministers of the United Methodist Church, being held in Pine Forest, Florida, USA. He requested prayer for healing, which was met with some consternation by those leading the conference. However, a few leaders volunteered to pray for him and, as they did so, the power of God fell on Craig. For a couple of hours he was on the floor while his stomach area gurgled and his body shook. Afterwards, Craig felt really hungry and proceeded to the fellowship hall along with the other leaders attending the conference. He gobbled down some food and digested it with his newly-replaced-and-restored stomach! For the last twelve years Craig has enjoyed the blessing of a normally-functioning, albeit miraculously recreated, stomach.

Healing missions

While on heaven's operating table in Florida, Craig was certain that he had heard the Lord say to him, 'I am the same yesterday, today and forever. I am the Lord who heals. Arise and eat, for you are healed. Freely you have received, freely you are to give. Pray for the sick and just see that I will confirm by signs, wonders and miracles.' So, armed with his own miraculous healing plus a sense of divine commission, Craig and Jenni asked the Lord to open doors for them to preach the Gospel and to pray for the sick. Once more their prayers were answered. In July 2000 a week-long series of meetings at Gracewood United Methodist Church in Augusta, Georgia, turned into 40 continuous days of meetings, as God poured out his Holy Spirit on the congregation. This was immediately followed by five weeks of meetings at the Washington, Georgia, Church of God.

In the subsequent years, successful mission meetings followed in New Zealand, Australia, Spain, Ibiza, Belgium, South Africa, Germany and England, as well as the United States. Often plans for several evenings of services turned into several weeks of meetings. In Surrey, a woman got out of a wheelchair in response to prayer. In New Zealand in 2002, a blind man's sight was restored. In the first five years of the new millennium, thousands had come into a saving knowledge of Jesus Christ and thousands more had found their healing as the Lord touched their lives.

Steps of faith

As Lloyd met Craig and Jenni Marsh in Southampton and listened to their story, therefore, he felt a divine impulse to invite them to consider visiting Stoke-on-Trent. Having indicated their willingness to do so, a church leaders' lunch was held at Bethel Christian Centre on Wednesday 13 July 2005, when Craig and Jenni met 25 local pastors in order to explore together the idea of a city-wide healing mission. There being a consensus in favour of holding such meetings, work began in earnest to prepare for the event. Time-scales were tight, because the proposed mission would be held over 12 evenings commencing in late September 2005. The venue was to be a large static marquee at local beauty spot and visitor attraction Trentham Gardens. The meetings were to go under the title 'A time for healing.'

A large amount of work was accomplished in the two months between the Christian leaders' first meeting with Craig and Jenni and the launch of the mission. Church leaders and churches involved in the 2C7 journey were invited to commit prayer, finance and volunteers to the mission. From among the participating churches, teams of stewards, musicians and intercessors were recruited, as well as helpers to deal with those who would enquire about Christian commitment and to pray for those who requested prayers for healing. Significant attention was paid to training the teams of volunteers. Local Christian leaders took responsibility over specific areas of work, making the large task achievable.

Saltbox administrator John Naylor, with the help of local Anglican Peter Morrallee, supervised the stewards. Elim Church pastors Phil and Sue Parsons, with Anglican vicar Sue Goodwin, trained and supervised the response team. Nigel di Castiglione, vicar of Trentham, supported by Rural Dean Will Slater and Methodist minister William Porter, organised those praying for the sick. Methodist ministers

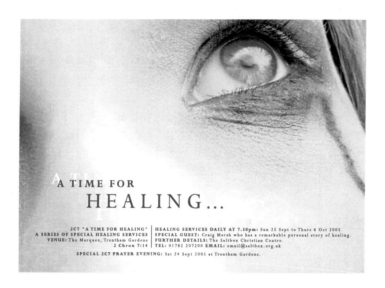

Ian and Liz Duffy, along with Geoff and Val Hesbrook, prepared and led a team of intercessors.

Alongside this, much work was done to prepare seating and staging for the marquee, sound and vision for the services, hospitality for guests, signing for the profoundly deaf and a bookstall for the benefit of all. A budget of £32,000 was set for the event, which represented a large step of faith, notwithstanding the generous support of participating churches. Publicity was undertaken by the Saltbox through the means of local churches, Cross Rhythms City Radio, the Sentinel newspaper and a large banner at the entrance to Trentham Gardens.

A time for healing

Very soon the opening of the mission arrived. The first meeting took place on the evening of Sunday 25 September 2005. More than 750 people from across North Staffordshire and beyond were in attendance, representing a magnificent turnout for the opening meeting. Craig shared his amazing story of healing, before inviting people to respond for prayer. Hundreds filed forwards in response to the invitation and prayer was offered for each and every person by Craig and Jenni, as well as the local trained volunteers.

From that superb start, the mission moved on in strength, inspiration and excitement. Numbers dipped to 500 on the Monday evening, but rose again on the Tuesday. On Wednesday evening some 900 people were present. The increased attendance may have been helped by a very positive report about the mission which appeared in the Sentinel newspaper on Wednesday 28 September, as well as by the contagious impact of word-of-mouth.

The format of the mission meetings was intentionally simple. Each evening either Lloyd or I welcomed the people and set the stage for the meeting. There followed a time of worship, which was supported by teams of local Christian musicians, skillfully and sensitively led by the faithful 2C7 worship leader Paul Critchley. To engage in worship at such meetings is so important, for these occasions are not essentially about human friendship and corporate encouragement, but about meeting with the living God. The stage having been set, Craig would then speak about his own experience of life and healing, combined with the promises of God's saving help found in the Bible. This would lead for an invitation to those not yet believers in Jesus to consider becoming followers of Christ. Finally, an invitation was made to those wishing to receive prayer for physical and emotional infirmity.

A tidal wave of blessing

In view of the numbers in attendance and the strong receptivity at work among the congregations, any and every invitation made resulted in a large number of respondents. At those moments all the preparatory hard work of prayer, organisation and training paid handsome dividends. Even with such a good support network, the task of praying for the sick often took a couple of hours at the conclusion of each meeting. But it was not simply about praying for the sick to find healing. Paul Critchley and his band led worship not just at the commencement of the meetings, but for up to three hours at the end as well. Their sensitive and spiritual ministry facilitated an atmosphere of awe and wonder in the presence of God.

This sense of awe increased as the mission progressed, just as the numbers in attendance increased even further during the second week of meetings. There was a sense of God at work, not just with individuals, but also with the corporate body of believers. It is impossible to describe in words the holy and joyful atmosphere contained in the mission meetings. Too soon the evenings flew by and too soon the mission drew to its conclusion.

Although there was some criticism in some quarters about the style and substance of the meetings, the overall sense was strongly in favour of proceeding with the mission beyond the scheduled closing date. Craig and Jenni Marsh were among many who believed this to be the best course of action. However, Lloyd and I, in conjunction with local church leaders, took the decision to stop the mission on the scheduled date of Thursday 6 October 2005 and to prepare to re-launch it in the spring of 2006. This would allow for proper preparations and necessary arrangements to be made. This decision was duly announced on the last of the 12 nights of meetings, a mission which had been almost without precedent in North Staffordshire.

Stories of healing

To think that the content of the mission meetings consisted merely of enthusiasm and excitement, however, would be way off target. Certainly the inspiration, uplift and impact of the meetings was much better experienced than can be adequately described on paper. Yet, each evening, the acts of worship were sincere, the declarations of the message of the Bible were clear and challenging, and the stories of healing in answer to prayer genuine.

Whilst not being able to document and describe the positive outcomes of the mission in detail, the following documented stories arising from the mission at least provide a flavour of the wonderful achievements of the meetings.

At one mission meeting, 'Alison'[1] received prayer regarding two lumps in her throat, which were the result of an overactive thyroid gland. The lumps having disappeared, 'Alison' had

---

[1] This and all other names have been changed in order to protect those involved. I have in my possession the written accounts of all these stories of healing.

visited her doctor, who could not understand or explain why this should be so. She had now come off the medication she had been taking. 'Jane' had taken a cloth that had been prayed over in the mission meeting and had placed it on a man suffering with a cancerous tumour. The man was overjoyed to report that the tumour had shrunk drastically. 'Jenny' reported that both her teenage daughter and her daughter's friend had become Christians during the mission.

'Andrew' recorded a vision he had seen during his church prayer meeting, which had coincided with the last night of the 'Time for healing' mission. In the dream, he had seen 'a river of crystal clear water flowing through the tent, out of the tent, out through the churches into the city. This river was a river of God's pure, unpolluted love reaching the whole of the city.' This seems a fitting picture with which to summarise the outstanding 'Time for healing' mission of 2005. Hundreds were encouraged and uplifted. Scores were transformed and healed. Christians across the area had successfully co-operated to make the mission happen. And every expense was met, with money left over with which to launch part two in the Spring of 2006.

Intensive preparations

Almost immediately, the work of preparation for part two of the mission commenced. Numerous planning meetings took place over the autumn and winter. A month of prayer was planned for February 2006, in order to prepare the ground for the mission. Four weeks of meetings were scheduled in March and April 2006. A budget of over £70,000 was set. The new mission was to be entitled 'A touch of heaven' because the emphasis was to be placed not only on the healing of sick people, but on receiving the anointing of God's spirit and experiencing heaven's restoring and reviving power.

The new mission was to be different in another very important aspect, too. The first two weeks would be held in the marquee at Trentham Gardens, while the following two weeks would be located in four different venues around North Staffordshire, with three evenings in each of the four venues. In this way it was hoped to begin to disseminate and give away the blessing of the mission to North Staffordshire, rather than to attempt to hold it all in one central place.

Once more the intercessors, 18 stewards, 64 response team members, worship team members and 71 prayer team members required recruiting and training. Once again the seating, staging, lighting and sound had to be arranged. Alongside the practical arrangements, the month of prayer provided a level of spiritual preparation.

On this occasion 29 churches and organisations committed to the month of prayer, one group more than enough to cover the 28 days of the month. In terms of denominational background, the 29 participating groups were Anglican, Methodist, Baptist, Salvation Army, United Reformed Church, Assemblies of God, Elim Pentecostal and independent charismatic. From a geographic perspective, the 29 groups were mainly based in Stoke-on-Trent and Newcastle-under-Lyme, plus one church each in the towns of Congleton, Leek, Stone, Uttoxeter and Rugeley.

A touch of heaven
The second healing mission opened with an evening of prayer in the marquee at Trentham on Monday 6 March 2006. The mission proper began on Tuesday 7 March, running until Sunday 12 March, before taking a night's break and running for six more evenings from 14 – 19 March. Being early March, the evenings were still relatively dark. That particular March, the weather was also unusually cold.

'A touch of heaven' was an accurate title to describe the mission meetings, though the numbers were unexpectedly low during the first week. By the second week, however, attendance had increased significantly and the blessing of God was being experienced to such an extent that conversations were held about extending the mission beyond the four scheduled weeks.

Once again the stories of God's intervention in answer to prayer were many and varied. 'Philippa' had experience terrible sexual abuse as a child, leading to crippling emotions of guilt and self-loathing. Receiving prayer at a mission meeting, she received a deep peace and cleansing. She described it later as though cleansing water had been poured over her until she was completely pure and whole. 'Dawn' reported that a lump in her right breast had disappeared in answer to prayer, a fact confirmed by medical examination. 'Alan' wrote about having been set free from long-standing issues of violent temper and severe mood swings, which had arisen because he had experienced rejection in childhood.

Divine intervention
After two weeks in the marquee at Trentham Gardens, the meetings relocated to Kidsgrove, close to the Cheshire border. The power of God present in the meetings was increasing and on one of the three evenings in Kidsgrove, a lady involuntarily began to show that she was demonised. This was evident through her facial expressions, verbal responses and involuntary movements. When the Spirit of God is released, there can often be a spiritual response from the powers of evil. The tormented lady found freedom in Jesus Christ that evening.

A further pressure at that time was the projected severe financial shortfall for the four weeks of mission. The free-will offerings were good and the support from local churches excellent, but the budget was high. An emergency meeting was held on Tuesday 28 March and the matter committed to prayer. It was also arranged to ask the church leaders connected to 2C7 to meet prior to the mission meeting in Burslem on Friday 31 March. This meeting took place as arranged, but it did not proceed as envisaged. For, while I had imagined that I would be asking the pastors for financial help, I was able to report three gifts of £5,000 each donated in the three intervening days! The effect of this injection of £15,000 was to remove the projected shortfall and to restore the mission to financial stability. Another very different answer to prayer by divine intervention....

The mission moved on from Kidsgrove to Burslem, where the three evenings spent at the Queen's Theatre witnessed an unfolding of God's presence that was tangible and which demanded a response of adoration, faith and surrender. The meetings began at 7.30pm and concluded at midnight, with three hours each evening of prayer, worship, crying and laughter, release and amazement in God's presence.

New heights

Week four of the 'Touch of heaven' mission ran over five evenings from Wednesday 5 to Sunday 9 April 2006 inclusive. The venue for these five nights was Bethel Christian Centre, the spiritual home of the 2C7 prayer movement. Its building was large and suitable, its leaders welcoming. Up to 500 people attended the meetings that week, with the spiritual bar raised, the worship full, the invitations to discipleship clear and the responses overwhelming.

Friday 7 April stands out in my mind very vividly. Craig and Jenni Marsh announced a 'sheep dip,' something with which they, as New Zealanders, were very familiar. This particular sheep dip consisted of a line of pray-ers standing side by side along the front of the meeting hall, with another line standing side-by-side facing the first. As each pray-er stretched their hands out towards each other a human tunnel was created. Each member of the congregation was invited to walk through the prayer tunnel while the intercessors in the lines on either side prayed for them. A few people did make it through the prayer tunnel still on their feet, but the majority did not. Such was the power of God in evidence, that most people began to walk through the tunnel, but ended up on the floor long before they reached the other end.

At the end of the four remarkable weeks, on Sunday 9 April I announced that the mission would continue after a two-week break over the forthcoming Holy Week and Easter Week. The reasons for the break were to allow church members to participate in their own Easter-focused events and to make some space for a rest, because many of us were exhausted.

Glory released

This tiredness was not just a physical response to the long meetings night after night over four weeks, but from the draining effect of the spiritual battles inevitably being fought behind the scenes at such missions. Those who have never carried responsibility for such missions can never imagine the intensity of such spiritual warfare. Those who have done so can never forget. On Wednesday 26 April, the regular monthly 2C7 prayer meeting heralded the recommencement of the healing mission. Over four nights from Thursday to Sunday inclusive, Lloyd and I led the meetings, brought a message from the Bible and introduced the time of prayer. For by this time, Craig and Jenni were leading a mission elsewhere.

Four more nights of mission took place at the Bethel Christian Centre from Thursday 4 – Sunday 7 May, then four more from Thursday 11 – Sunday 14 May, and a final four from Thursday 18 – Sunday 21 May 2006. Craig and Jenni came back to lead some of the meetings, but most took place in their absence. Their work, in a sense, had been completed, the fires lit and the glory of God's presence released. Finally, after 45 nights of prayer, worship and healing spread over eight weeks, the 'Touch of heaven' mission drew to a conclusion, having touched hundreds of people and lifted our hearts to heaven, even as heaven had reached down to touch us.

10: SIGNS OF HOPE

The healing missions of 2006 and 2007 made a remarkable and, in some cases, life-changing impression on the lives of many people in Stoke-on-Trent and beyond. The impact of the 2C7 journey did not end there, however. While not wanting to claim for 2C7 more than is due, the prayer movement provided an environment in which Christian leaders, people, churches and organisations found inspiration, encouragement, enrichment, focus and momentum.

Invigorated leaders

The 2C7 Christian leaders' prayer meetings proved to be a place where God, by the means of his Holy Spirit, spoke clearly and directly to leaders on a regular basis. The way in which this divine interchange happened varied from person to person, but the result was consistent – a renewed focus and a re-invigorated ministry.

In 2002, Rev. Mick Ellor, team vicar in the Bucknall Parish, was tired and dejected, leading him to make the decision to leave the area at the end of his contract and to relocate to an 'easier parish' elsewhere. At a 2C7 meeting in the summer of 2002, however, the Lord met with Mick. As a result of this divine encounter, Mick and his wife Jan knew that they had to stay in Stoke-on-Trent and continue their work. This they duly did. Mick became Rector of the Parish and served there for a further seven years, bringing renewal and new growth to the churches.

Methodist minister Ian Duffy remembers the early years of 2C7 for the considerable personal spiritual growth which was stimulated within him and his wife Liz. He was especially touched by the corporate prayer for the needs of the conurbation. In Ian's own words:

It was great to meet with hundreds of people from all denominations who felt the need to gather in prayer for the city (and beyond). It felt as if we were unified in spirit with so many like-minded people. It was good to gather in the smaller groups on the Wednesday evenings. It broke down barriers and helped to make us more aware of the people of God around the city. The praying out loud was an eye-opener for some, but enabled us to develop more in our own prayer-life.[1]

In 2005, Ian and Liz moved on to the Witney Methodist Circuit in Oxfordshire. For four years they led a united prayer gathering in Faringdon using the principles of 2C7 that they had learned in Stoke-on-Trent, inviting secular leaders to address gatherings of Christians to enable united prayers for God's blessing on the local community.

Purposeful fellowship

Rev. John Titlow arrived in Staffordshire just after the birth of the 2C7 prayer journey, with the remit of stimulating mission among four local United Reformed Church congregations. John's perspective on the prayer meetings is illuminating:

The 2C7 meetings provided me with the opportunity to meet with others who had a concern for a making a difference in Jesus' name for the benefit of the whole community. It was easy to become isolated in a

---

[1] E-mail from Ian and Liz Duffy, 3 June 2011.

denominational box, and to feel that the task was simply too great for one individual or tradition. The worship offered in the 2C7 meetings soon linked me in with God's perspective and the prayer concerns made it clear that God has an agenda for the area - and that we are all, together, part of it.

Apart from the strategic links that were formed among those working to see God's Kingdom come, there has been a tremendous sense of anticipation that the Lord would move across the area. In my own ministry I have begun to see evidence of this, almost always when working in co-operation with different streams and traditions. Without the support, the input from national and international speakers, and the God-encounters provided by 2C7, I feel I would have lost hope many years ago.[2]

Pastors Phil and Sue Parsons have served as leaders of Longton Elim Church for 35 years. Phil shares in common with John Titlow the recollection of a renewed sense of city-wide purpose that the prayer journey released:

2C7 was a powerful prayer movement that brought believers together from various denominations in a strong sense of unity of purpose to see the area impacted by a move of the Spirit of God. Many prayers were answered, some quite spectacularly, and the prayer movement cultivated a sense of direction and momentum that resulted in the creation or encouragement of evangelism and mercy ministries. Speaking personally and on behalf of our congregation who were committed to it, 2C7 was a time of rich fellowship, exciting praise and worship, and encouraging information for prayer and

[2]E-mail from John Titlow, 24 July 2011.
[3]E-mail from Phil Parsons, 4 August 2011.

praise. It had an impact that touched the lives of many people in public life and was a positive witness to the movers and shakers of the city and beyond.[3]

Potter's House

In April 1991, after four years of prayer and preparation, a church plant was born out of the historic Swan Bank Methodist Mission in Burslem. The new church eventually settled in the Birches Head area of the city and experienced slow-but-steady growth through the 1990s. Through his connection with 2C7, church leader Pastor Phil Barber believes that he and the church were able to move to a new level of blessing and progress.

In November 2005, the Birches Head Christian Fellowship purchased a complete redundant high school building and refurbished it to be a centre where start-up businesses, community groups and the church could share common space and build bridges. The aptly-named Bridge Centre has been a success story ever since its opening in January 2007, providing a home for numerous businesses, the Stoke-on-Trent City Music School and a nursery. It is also used extensively by community groups, for training events, conferences and concerts.

The church experienced significant growth throughout the 2C7 period, leading to the need for two Sunday morning meetings to accommodate the congregation of more than 400 people. In 2006 Birches Head Christian Fellowship was renamed The Potter's House, with the subtitle '21st Century Church,' to reflect its aim to be culturally relevant and forward looking.

Sleeping giants awakened

Abbey Hulton's Bethel Christian Centre served as the home base for almost all the events and meetings held under the auspices of the 2C7 movement throughout its seven years of existence. The building was eminently suitable for the purpose, having a large auditorium, modern layout, adequate heating, a sound and vision system, and a large car park. The premises were made freely available to us by the generosity of the leaders of the church.

However, for a number of reasons the local church congregation was not itself experiencing great success during this period. Things were to change, however, when James and Becky Galloway became church leaders on 1 September 2007. James had grown up in Knypersley in the Staffordshire Moorlands, but spent his adult years in the East Midlands and South Wales before returning 'home' to North Staffordshire to lead Bethel Christian Centre. James and Becky made an immediate impact at the church and, in a remarkably short period of time, ushered in a new season of growth within the context of a spiritual environment of renewed vision and faith. The sleeping giant was well and truly awakened.

Just one day before the Galloways took on the leadership of the church in Abbey Hulton, Methodist ministers Ashley and Moira Cooper were inducted to the leadership of Swan Bank Methodist Mission. 'Swan Bank' has a long and distinguished history within Methodism, having been founded by potters returning from the meetings held by John Wesley at Bristol in 1740. Since that time, it had played a central role in the town of Burslem, Stoke-on-Trent, the community which it serves.

Swan Bank Mission had experienced a challenging time in the early years of the 21st Century, but the arrival of Ashley and Moira was to mark a positive change in the situation and the beginning of a new season of rebuilding and growth. Through the dynamic and visionary leadership of Ashley and Moira, the sleeping giant which had been Swan Bank Mission was also awakened.

127

For much of its existence, the Hanley Assemblies of God congregation had met in a church building originally erected in the 19th Century to house a group of Welsh Congregationalists. In 2003, the opportunity arose for the church to partner with the Stoke-on-Trent City Council in a completely new building that would incorporate a meeting place for the church, plus a café, nursery and gym. The impressive, prominently-located building overlooks the city centre of Stoke-on-Trent. Long-standing church leader Patrick Parkes shared the vision of the Hope Centre in the context of several 2C7 leaders' prayer meetings and publicly acknowledged that the new operating environment in Stoke-on-Trent, connecting as it did the spiritual and the socio-political, was a major feature in the successful realisation of the vision of the Hope Centre.[4]

Churches planted

The 2C7 prayer movement was enriched by its connection to a number of church plants which came into being in the mid-2000s. Anthony and Gill Henson arrived from Leicester in the summer of 2003 to plant a New Frontiers Church in the area. Grace Church reached out to students and young people, meeting initially in rooms belonging to Staffordshire University in Shelton. A strong group was established and continues, though the Hensons moved to Lincoln in January 2008 in order to plant a New Frontiers Church there.

Southern Africans Gordon and Judy Crowther relocated from the Lake District to Stoke-on-Trent in 2003 at the invitation of Christopher Hill, Bishop of Stafford. Ordained vicar Gordon was appointed to engage in a completely new

---

[4]Sadly, the community aspect of the Hope Centre project was to fail in the medium-term, but the fact remains that 2C7 played a role in the birth of the vision.

type of Anglican ministry. His sphere of ministry was not to be a traditional parish, but people in the 20-40 age group across the conurbation. The experimental 'Church Without Walls' was established and continued to meet in the City Centre. Gordon and Judy moved back to South Africa in 2009 in order to take on the leadership of The Church of the Holy Spirit, a large Anglican parish in Capetown.

The Chelmsford-based Christian Growth Centre planted a church in the Meir Park area of the city in early 2008. Martin and Alison Macklin, who had been involved in the leadership of the mother church in Chelmsford, were led to relocate to Stoke in order to start a new congregation. 'Christian Growth Centre Stoke' made its home in St Clare's Centre, a building belonging to the Church of England, but no longer being used by the Anglican congregation. From this base, the new church is reaching out into the community in the Meir and Meir Park areas of the city.

Minority ethnic congregations

The early years of the 21st Century also witness the planting of several minority ethnic churches in Stoke-on-Trent, reflecting the national trend and adding variety and energy to the kingdom of God in the conurbation. Connections and relationships were established with and between these congregations and their leaders. Among the plants were a Chinese congregation led by Erik and Hedy Lee and a Burslem-based Fijian congregation led by Aselah Waqa. The American-born Church of God (Seventh Day) was introduced into the Potteries by Hughie and Angela Lawrence at the turn of the Millennium. The main thrust of their ministry locally is training and partnership work, specifically, though not exclusively, within the Black and Minority Ethnic communities.

Two congregations have been established in the city from a Nigerian base. The Christ Triumphant Chapel is based in

Burslem and is led by Pastor John Appiah. A local expression of a huge Nigerian denomination, the Redeemed Christian Church of God, was planted in 2003 in the town of Stoke. The church is called Living Waters Parish and its leaders are Dr. Marcus and Mrs. Norah Chilaka.

Radio stations

Alongside local churches, the 2C7 journey has been enhanced by, and has added value into, its two locally-based Christian radio stations. United Christian Broadcasters has been based in North Staffordshire since it was planted in 1986. The early years of the 21st Century have, however, been a time of significant development in the ministry of the ministry. The huge strides forward have included the launching of a television channel, covering the UK with a DAB digital radio station and the acquisition of a second office building in Stoke-on-Trent. It was a privilege to welcome United Christian Broadcasters staff members at many 2C7 prayer events, to pray with them for the success of the ministry and to partner with them in days and weeks of prayer. United Christian Broadcasters has been, and remains, a gift to and from North Staffordshire, influencing thousands for the Gospel across Europe and beyond.

As we have seen, Cross Rhythms City Radio has enjoyed a close relationship with 2C7 from the early days of both movements in the city. Launching in February 2002 at a 2C7 prayer event, Cross Rhythms found a base in the old Radio Stoke buildings in the City Centre. The ministry has been through many challenging times, but has survived and flourished by God's grace. Former leaders Chris and Kerry Cole, and current leaders Jonathan and Heather Bellamy, have maintained a close working relationship with the 2C7 journey and its leaders. The radio station has built for itself a niche among local civic and political leaders, from which it is able to reflect city issues alongside Christian music and ministry in a unique blend. Increasingly Cross Rhythms has gained a role as a model for similar community radio stations in the UK and beyond.

The Saltbox

Through director Lloyd Cooke and administrator John Naylor, the Saltbox played a central role in the birth and life of the 2C7 movement. It also experienced dramatic growth during the 2C7 years in response to its involvement in the prayer movement. One specific trigger of change was the employment of Linda Williams in 2006 to conduct a Faith Action Audit of the community work undertaken by people involved in faith communities in Stoke-on-Trent. By means of an extensive survey carried out among the churches and other faith communities in the city, it became clear that faith group members (mainly Christians) engaged in a staggeringly large amount of community work in a whole variety of ways. The highlight finding of the Faith Action Audit was that members of the 154 faith communities in Stoke-on-Trent gave more than 5,000 hours in voluntary service in their neighbourhoods each week, an amount of time commitment equating to 130 full-time jobs.[5]

As a result of the survey, in 2007 Saltbox was able to gain favour and funding to employ both an older people's and a younger people's networker. In the event, the young people's aspect of the work did not develop, but the older people's exceeded expectations. Under the leadership of Ann Chatwin, connections were made with local church senior

[5]This voluntary service did not take into account time given by faith community members to activities which benefitted their own place of worship. Figures are taken from Stoke-on-Trent Faith Action

citizens groups on the one side, and resource providers on the other. Other specific initiatives have sprung from those connections and continue to thrive.

In addition to Ann and Linda's community work, Lloyd was consistently building relationships with political, civic, business and community leaders in the city and beyond. This led to him taking a seat on the city's Local Strategic Partnership board as a faith representative. This in turn led to many other strategic opportunities, such as chairing the Staffordshire Consortium of Infrastructure Organisations and engagement with many groups and organisations. The influence gained through such connections has been invaluable.

Beacon House of Prayer

William and Karen Porter moved to Stoke-on-Trent in 2003, quickly becoming an integral part of 2C7 journey. Through Martin Scott's prophetic ministry in November 2003, they became convinced that their calling was to re-dig the wells of revival in the city for the blessing of the city – and the nation. This calling began to take on life and form in 2005 and 2006, in a vision to build a house of prayer. The word they believe they received from the Lord was, 'I want you to build me a house of radical worship, teaching and prayer, where the lost will be saved, the sick healed, the downtrodden raised up and my glory revealed. And it shall be a holy house, a light on a hill, marked by my presence, which you will carry to the nations.'

William and Karen, in league with Paul and Tracy Critchley and others, launched the Beacon House of Prayer and Christian Fellowship in October 2007, using the Packmoor Community Centre as a base for their Sunday morning meetings and renting a house in Sandyford in order to allow

Audit, published by the Saltbox Christian Centre, 2006.

for ongoing prayer during the week. The ministry of worship and prayer increased by leaps and bounds through 2007 and 2008. From small beginnings, the ministry and influence of the Beacon House of Prayer increased dramatically. More and more space has been rented, and the Sunday meetings relocated to the Sandyford Base. An unbroken prayer ministry became quickly and strongly established, focusing on the city, rather than on the Beacon's own needs or desires. This in turn added to the prayer output for the conurbation. The Beacon House of Prayer quickly became a very important partner on the journey in the latter stages of 2C7 – and into the era beyond.

By God's grace, the visionary prayer, corporate journey, meaningful relationships and shared experiences of God's presence helped to change the direction and destiny of individuals, local churches and faith organisations. Many in Stoke-on-Trent, and well beyond its borders, can testify to the life-transforming encounters with God and with other people through the hub that 2C7 became. In God's plan, everybody was a winner.

11: FROM SILVER TO GOLD

Entering 2008, the city-focused prayer meetings were continuing on a monthly basis. The number of leaders meeting to pray averaged 50, while the numbers attending the open prayer meetings on the last Wednesday of the month hovered around the 120 mark. The vision of city transformation was still clear and the relationships among leaders and people were still strong.

Neutral facilitation

Lloyd and I still carried the vision and leadership of the movement. We had discovered that leadership within the context of an inter-church, city-wide movement differs in significant ways from the leadership required in a local church environment or in an organisational setting. In this wider sphere, leadership must be even more facilitative, maintaining the balance between having a sense of direction and incorporating the vision of fellow-leaders, because many of the fellow-travellers on the journey are themselves strong characters, gifted leaders and anointed visionaries.

Then the leadership of a corporate movement is relational. Both Lloyd and I belonged to local churches within established denominations throughout the 2C7 time-period, but neither of us functioned as denominational representatives in our facilitation of the 2C7 journey. Our authority was not based on structural hierarchy or denominational position. Leadership was granted to us by the church leaders, not demanded from them by us. A further important factor in facilitative leadership is credibility. The credibility we had established arose from many years of investment in relationships with Christian and secular leaders, from the long-term support and help we had offered others and from our evident commitment to the goal of the transformation of North Staffordshire.

Another challenging tension of leadership is that of holding tightly to the vision in order to protect it from corruption and deviation, whilst holding lightly to structures and forms, which are transitory and changeable. And the vision must always be held in submission to the Lord, because he is the ultimate source of authority and head of the church.

Mutual accountability

Some may imagine a certain *kudos* attached to the leadership role exercised in large gatherings as well as in private meetings with highly influential people. From our perspective, it was about significance more than prominence, about influence rather than control, about vision more than structure. And those who have been leaders know that there is always a high cost to leadership.

Not everyone was always content with the decisions taken or words spoken by Lloyd and me. Occasional letters of complaint arrived on our desks. Some thought our leadership too strong; others that it was too weak. Several were concerned about our teaching; others about the perceived influence of other leaders over us. Such criticism was overall a positive thing, in that it caused us to see things from a different perspective. As Solomon in his wisdom wrote so long ago, 'Wounds from a friend can be trusted' (Proverbs 27:6).

And it would be wrong to think that Lloyd and I acted with no reference to other people. We were at every stage of the journey blessed with the support and advice of a team of local church leaders. This arrangement never took on a formal structure, but the team relationships were strong, the meetings robust and the accountability real. In the early days of the journey, when everything was so new, the prayer meetings so vibrant and the numbers involved so large, there was a great need to meet at least once per month to reflect on what had happened and pray over what was going to happen.

A team simply dubbed a 'working party' consisted of Lloyd, Paul Critchley (worship leader), John Naylor (Saltbox administrator), four local church leaders and me. By 2005 this had given way to a smaller team of five people, who explored over an 18-monthperiodthe concept of what a 'city eldership' might look like and how it might function. This group, and the vision it explored together, did not in the event develop or last, and by January 2007 a new 'advisory group' of 12 people became the custodians of the vision and its outworking for the remainder of the 2C7 period.

Alongside the prayer and conversation of friends, prophetic words were often submitted during the prayer meetings and between meetings. These were always taken seriously and prayed over. On some occasions they proved to be extremely relevant concerning a specific need or situation.

All movements require administrative and financial support, especially when crowds of people, publicity, buildings and finances are involved. It is impossible to overestimate the part that Saltbox administrator John Naylor played in this. John paid meticulous attention to detail, had a wide experience of business, lots of financial ability and great common sense. These natural gifts were matched by his ability to see the vision and travel the journey with us in every respect. John's complete reliability and trustworthiness, coupled with a servant heart, made him the ideal administrative supporter.

A grain of wheat

On just one or two occasions during the seven-year journey of prayer we seriously considered bringing the public prayer meetings to a close. Each time we pondered whether to do this, however, a fresh impetus of life and energy seemed to ignite among leaders and people. Then, suddenly and unexpectedly, in October 2008 the Lord spoke very clearly to us about bringing the 2C7 brand and meetings to a conclusion. This took place at one of the Connecting the Connectors conferences in Swanwick, Derbyshire, which Lloyd and I were helping to facilitate.

During the conference, someone spoke about it being a new season, in which the old and existing had to be laid down in order for the new to arise. Among all the words spoken over the three days of meeting, that one phrase leapt out and impacted Lloyd, myself and one or two other 2C7 leaders present. In a moment we knew that we had to 'sow the grain of wheat into the ground'[1] to die, so that an even bigger crop of blessing could grow up in due time. The concept is simple enough. We understand that sowing seeds into the ground in autumn will lead to shoots coming up in the spring, flowers in the summer and fruit at the harvest. However, this necessitates a real step of faith at the point of sowing into the ground. At that point, the grain of wheat is all we have. We have to believe that losing what we have will result in something much bigger and better emerging at the right time. But at the time of sowing, there are no guarantees. This is where we stood on 8 October 2008.

The end of the beginning

In response to the moment of revelation, those of us present at the conference in Swanwick held an impromptu

---

[1] These words of Jesus can be found in John 12:24.

conversation and decided to consult the 2C7 advisory team about the future. This meeting was held on Tuesday 21 October, when a lengthy and in-depth discussion took place concerning the way ahead. The corporate decision of the advisory team was to lay down the Wednesday evening city prayer meetings, together with the 2C7 name and brand. However, it was agreed to continue to meet as leaders on retreat at Shallowford House, to reconvene another Embrace worship day and to continue with the months of unbroken prayer as before.

This decision was to be announced at the 2C7 meetings coming up just a week later, on Monday 27 and Wednesday 29 October 2008. As it happened, the meeting of Wednesday 29 October represented the completion of almost exactly seven years from the commencement of the 2C7 journey. The announcements made at the leaders' and public prayer meetings were met with a great deal of surprise and sadness. Among the many comments made and e-mails received, however, a strong sense of acceptance, of thankfulness and of expectation for the future came through. Two hundred people gathered for a final thanksgiving meeting which was held on Wednesday 25 November 2008.The 2C7 era had finished.

God's gracious pause
In bringing the 2C7 era to a close, it was not as though we had lost our vision for the healing of the land, or were ending our long-standing commitment to the transformation of Stoke-on-Trent. Rather, we had completed that particular leg of the journey and were leaving behind some structures, which, although very precious and helpful in their time, would now prove to be a great hindrance to the next leg of the journey, whose nature and scope were very different to what had brought us this far.

At a practical level, we agreed that the leaders' prayer meetings were to continue on the last Monday of each month, but were to relocate to the Bridge Centre and to be renamed 'Connect.' We believed that we were entering a holding pattern. We knew clearly where and what we had come from, but much less about where we were going, and could not claim to have entered the new season we were creating space for.

Therefore, using the name 'Connect' for the meetings and the Bridge Centre as a venue was pertinent and helpful in describing the nature of the new stage of the journey. We were to enter a period of gracious pause, between what was and what was to come. Such times are not times of emptiness, but are in fact rich in rest, in recharging the batteries, in anticipation and preparation for the future.

The church leaders met to pray at the end of January, February and March 2009. Another season of unbroken prayer carried us from winter to spring. This season of 40 days of prayer of fasting among and by the churches was timed to coincide with the season of Lent, beginning on 1 March and ending on Good Friday, 10 April 2009. Two and a half weeks later, on Monday 27 April, the leaders gathered to pray for the city. There were two visitors at the event, representing two very different roles and functions. Alan Turley, director of the Stoke-on-Trent Local Strategic Partnership, gave an update on progress being made in various areas of city life. Dr. Russ Parker, director of the internationally-acclaimed Acorn Christian Healing Foundation, brought a powerful message from the New Testament book of Ephesians.

Mining for gold
The prayer event may not, however, be remembered in the long term for the input given by Alan Turley and Russ Parker, although their respective messages were helpful and

relevant. What grabbed the attention on the morning, and ever since, was a strong prophetic word brought by one of the church leaders present. Phil Barber, pastor of the Potter's House Church, said the following:

> I see a picture of the entrance to a mine, like you would see in an old Western film, with mine car and railway tracks going into the mine. There were dusty miners with picks and shovels standing outside the entrance.
>
> Then the Lord said that we had been down the mine once and had worked a vein of silver for seven years. The silver had been refined and had the pure metal had prospered the city. Then in obedience to him we have had a period of rest. The Lord said that it is time to return to the mine and begin working again, wresting the precious metal from the earth. Only this time it is a vein of gold. And gold is mined differently than silver. I had a strong picture of miners hacking at the rock with their picks and gouging out the ore.

The impact of this prophetic picture in the meeting was immediate and deep. It would also prove to be lasting. Rev. Rod Clark, team vicar of Christ Church, Cobridge, responded by e-mail a few days later with the thought that, although it can be difficult to extract the gold from the rock, we mine with the knowledge that the deposit of gold is already there. This means that we work from a position of confidence, rather than in mere speculation and wild hope.

When a group of 17 leaders gathered on prayer retreat at Shallowford House a week later, part of the time was spent in prayer and conversation around the prophecy, wondering what it would mean to find gold. The theme was again picked up at the leaders' prayer meeting of Monday 29 June 2009, when the leaders spent time in group prayer and discussion to discern what the Lord was saying to us. Feedback from the various groups was circulated to all the pastors for information and prayer. Further e-mails around the theme of finding gold continued to circulate during July 2009, and the subject was again raised at the leaders' prayer meeting of Monday 27 July. Certainly our attention had been gained and our minds captivated by the vision of finding gold.

Staffordshire Hoard

The summer passed and September 2009 witnessed a new round of church programmes and activities, in line with the beginning of the new academic year. However, while relaxing on a beach in Brittany on Thursday 24 September, I received a text message from Lloyd, containing a brief message about the discovery of a priceless hoard of gold in a field in Staffordshire! Through the wonders of the media, the whole world was informed that day that the biggest and best hoard of Anglo-Saxon gold ever found has been discovered near Lichfield. Almost 1,500 items of silver and gold, many filled with intricate and beautiful patterns and precious jewels, had been recovered from a field, having been found by an amateur metal detectorist in early July.

Several things were of great interest and encouragement to us in relation to the discovery of silver and gold. Firstly and foremost, it was for us a wonderful sign in the ground, the realm of nature, to confirm and encourage us towards the spiritual prize of finding gold that we had been promised. And even though the actual find had been made in early July, over two months before the announcement to the world, this was still over two months after the original prophetic picture about mining for gold.

Some of the details surrounding the discovery were also awe-inspiring. Interviewed shortly after the hoard became public knowledge, farmer and landowner Terry Herbert spoke about the fact that the gold had been brought to the surface because he kept ploughing 'deeper and deeper,' a phrase entirely reminiscent of the blessing spoken at the end of each public 2C7 meeting for the previous seven years.

Then, all the items in the hoard had been items used in warfare, 'with the exception of three crosses' and a gold belt containing the words, in Latin, 'Rise up, LORD! May your enemies be scattered; may your foes flee before you' (Numbers 10:35). Thus the only words coming to us from the 7th Century were words of scriptural blessing as spoken by Moses over the people of Israel each time they moved camp on their journey to the Promised Land.

By divine arrangement, a second Embrace worship day had been scheduled to take place on Saturday 26 September 2009, two days after the public announcement of the discovery of the Staffordshire Hoard. And two days later, on Monday 28 September, the monthly leaders' prayer meeting took place. At both events, great encouragement was derived from the sign that the Lord was giving us concerning finding gold.

Releasing agent

By another divine coincidence, Lloyd, Paul Critchley and I had spent 24 hours in a prayer retreat for the royal family at Windsor Castle in mid-September 2009. There we had spent some time with Julie Brown, a Lincoln-based lady called to pray for the monarch and the nation. After the public announcement about the discovery of the Staffordshire Hoard ten days after the Windsor Castle event, Julie told us that she had something to share about releasing gold from the rock which can so often hold and hide it. So Julie visited the leaders' prayer meeting of Monday 26 October 2009 to recount the story of the years she had spent living near San Jose, California, in the area where the gold rush of 1849 had taken place.

When the surface gold had all been removed, there was a need to remove gold from the ore in which it was contained. The agent to do this was mercury, which was found in the rock cinnabar. The cinnabar rock, however, was at that point only obtainable from the Almaden mine in Spain, which was under the control of the Rothschild family. All that changed in 1863, however, when the largest ever deposit of cinnabar was discovered in the San Jose hills, close to the rock containing the gold that required liberating!

In a stroke, the power of European control over the New World was broken, and California and the Central American states were able to release their bountiful supplies of gold and to use the profits to build their nations. Julie concluded her presentation by giving us five pieces of cinnabar from the hills of California, with the prayer that we would find gold – and the means and agents to release the gold from the rocks that house it.

Let my people go!
On Saturday 9 January 2010, at a public meeting held at the Bridge Centre, we announced a year of release and encouraged God's people to go to their homes, schools and places of work to be the releasing agents through which the gold of the glory of God contained in the people of Stoke-on-Trent could be discovered and released. We had come to believe that the years of digging deeper in prayer had brought the gold of the glory of God close to the surface, waiting to be uncovered by God's people in the arena of daily life, in their relationships, their work, their prayer, their learning and their leisure activities.

The stories of how that is becoming reality are being written even now...

*Then Jesus said,
'Did I not tell you that if you believe,
you will see the glory of God?'*

(John 11:40)

RESOURCES

The individuals, churches and organisations listed here all appear in the pages of this book. The information is provided to enable follow-up reading and research.

CONGREGATIONS IN STOKE-ON-TRENT

For more information about the vision and ministry of the Beacon House of Prayer in Sandyford, Stoke-on-Trent, visit http://www.beaconhop.org

Bethel Christian Centre, former base of 2C7 meetings, has now been re-purposed and renamed Breathe City Church. More information available at http://www.breathecitychurch.com James Galloway has recently chronicled the story of the church since 2007 in the book *From beach hut to palace*, published by River Publishing, 2011.

Access information about the three churches which form the Church of England Bucknall Parish at http://www.bucknallteam.org.uk

Find out more about the historic Burslem Methodist Mission, known locally as Swan Bank Methodist Church, at http://www.swanbank.org.uk

The Meir Park-based Christian Growth Centre Stoke is profiled at http://www.cgcstoke.org

An introduction to Church Without Walls can be found at http://www.churchwow.co.uk

Find out more about the Parish of St Luke, Endon, at http:/
/www.endonstlukes.org.uk

Grace Church, Stoke, belongs to the New Frontiers
International denomination. Its online home is http://
www.gracechurch.xtn.org

The Living Waters Parish of the Redeemed Christian Church
of God meets in Stoke. More information at http://
www.rccglivingwater.org

Find out more about Longton Elim Church at http://
www.longton-elim.org.uk

The website of the Potter's House Methodist Church,
formerly known as Birches Head Christian Fellowship, is at
http://www.thepottershouse.eu. The Bridge Centre, home
of the Potter's House congregation and other enterprises,
is profiled at http://www.thebridgecentre.org.uk

The historic Church of England Parish of St Mary's, Trentham,
can be accessed at http://www.trenthamchurch.org.uk

ORGANISATIONS IN NORTH STAFFORDSHIRE AND SOUTH CHESHIRE

Bethesda Chapel, which played such a prominent part in
19th Century life in the Potteries, is currently being restored
to its former glory. Find out more at http://www.bethesda-
stoke.info

Cross Rhythms City Radio has a multitude of resources freely
available on its website http://www.crossrhythms.co.uk

The excellent Englesea Brook Chapel and Museum preserves
the story and records of the Primitive Methodist Connexion.
Visit http://www.engleseabrook-museum.org.uk for
information and directions.

Find out more about the extensive inter-church and community work facilitated by the Saltbox Christian Centre at http://www.saltbox.org.uk

Information about Shallowford House, the Lichfield Diocesan retreat and conference centre, can be found at http://www.shallowfordhouse.org

The Staffordshire Sentinel newspaper is available online at http://www.thisisstaffordshire.co.uk

Access to United Christian Broadcasters' radio and TV channels, plus many other resources, can be gained at http://www.ucb.co.uk

CHRISTIAN LEADERS

Paul and Tracy Critchley still play a leadership role in the areas of worship and prayer. Their ministry is accessible at http://www.presenceworship.com

Bob Dunnett continues to fulfil an influential teaching and prophetic role. His teaching is located at http://www.understandingthetimes.co.uk

An introduction to the testimony and ministry of evangelists Craig and Jenni Marsh is available at http://www.turningpointministries.info

Martin Scott's ongoing prophetic journey can be followed via http://www.3generations.eu Martin's inspiring book about city-focused prayer, *Sowing seeds for revival*, was published in 2001. This was followed in 2004 by *Impacting the city.* Both books were published by Sovereign World and both are well worth reading!

NATIONAL AND INTERNATIONAL AGENCIES

Information about the ministry of the Acorn Christian Healing Foundation is accessible at http://www.acornchristian.org Russ Parker's excellent book *Healing wounded history* addresses many of the issues facing churches, communities and cities in our day. It was published by Darton, Longman and Todd in 2001.

Communities which promote the understanding and practice of Celtic Christianity include the Community of Aidan and Hilda (http://www.aidanandhilda.org) and the Northumbria Community (http://northumbriacommunity.org). There are many books available that deal with the roots and rhythms of Celtic Christianity, and its relevance for today.

Visit http://www.ibti.org.uk for an introduction to the work of the International Bible Training Institute, Burgess Hill, West Sussex.

Redeeming our Communities is based in Manchester but works in many towns and cities in the UK. More information about their city-transforming work is available at http://www.redeemingourcommunities.org.uk Frank and Debra Green's book *City-changing prayer*, published by Kingsway in 2005, tells the story of Manchester's city-wide prayer journey. Debra's book *Redeeming our communities* relates inspiring stories of community transformation from cities around the United Kingdom. It was published by New Wine Press in March 2008.

The vision and international networks of Saturation Church Planting International are presented at http://scpi.org

The Transformations films are still available from the Seattle-based Sentinel Group at http://www.glowtorch.org

The training and networking vision of church planting group Together in Mission can be viewed at http:// www.togetherinmission.co.uk

Find out more about the World Prayer Centre at http:// www.worldprayer.org.uk